ATLANTIS

By **Lally Katz**

Currency Press,
Sydney

CURRENCY PLAYS

First published in 2017
by Currency Press Pty Ltd,
PO Box 2287, Strawberry Hills, NSW, 2012, Australia
enquiries@currency.com.au
www.currency.com.au

in association with Belvoir, Sydney

Copyright: *Atlantis* © Lally Katz, 2017.

COPYING FOR EDUCATIONAL PURPOSES
The Australian *Copyright Act 1968* (Act) allows a maximum of one chapter or 10% of this book, whichever is the greater, to be copied by any educational institution for its educational purposes provided that that educational institution (or the body that administers it) has given a remuneration notice to Copyright Agency Limited (CAL) under the Act.

For details of the CAL licence for educational institutions contact CAL, 11/66 Goulburn Street, Sydney, NSW, 2000; tel: within Australia 1800 066 844 toll free; outside Australia 61 2 9394 7600; fax: 61 2 9394 7601; email: info@copyright.com.au

COPYING FOR OTHER PURPOSES
Except as permitted under the Act, for example a fair dealing for the purposes of study, research, criticism or review, no part of this book may be reproduced, stored in a retrieval system, or transmitted in any form or by any means without prior written permission. All enquiries should be made to the publisher at the address above.

Any performance or public reading of *Atlantis* is forbidden unless a licence has been received from the author or the author's agent. The purchase of this book in no way gives the purchaser the right to perform the play in public, whether by means of a staged production or a reading. All applications for public performance should be addressed to The Yellow Agency, PO Box 164, Erskineville NSW 2043, Australia; email: contact@theyellowagency.com

Cataloguing-in-publication data for this title is available from the National Library of Australia website: www.nla.gov.au

Typeset by Dean Nottle for Currency Press.
Cover design by Alphabet Studio.
Image shows Lucia Mastrantone, Amber McMahon & Paula Arundell.
Photography by Daniel Boud.

Contents

ATLANTIS

Act One	1
Act Two	15
Act Three	46
Act Four	65

Theatre Program at the end of the playtext

Currency Press acknowledges the Traditional Owners of the Country on which we live and work. We pay our respects to all Aboriginal and Torres Strait Islander Elders, past and present.

Atlantis was first produced by Belvoir at Belvoir St Theatre, Sydney, on 1 November 2017, with the following cast:

ELECTRA	Paula Arundell
BELLA / DOSSIE / NEW YORK TAXI DRIVER	Lucia Mastrantone
LALLY	Amber McMahon
DIEGO / PANTHER	Hazem Shammas
DAVE / POP-OP / BELLA'S DAUGHTER	Matthew Whittet

Minor roles were shared between the cast members.

Director, Rosemary Myers
Set and Costume Designer, Jonathon Oxlade
Lighting Designer, Damien Cooper
Composer and Sound Designer, Harry Covill
Dialect Coach, Paige Walker
Movement Director, Sara Black
Production Manager, Sally Withnell
Technical Manager, Aiden Brennan
Deputy Production Manager, Roxzan Bowes
Stage Manager, Keiren Smith
Assistant Stage Manager, Georgiane Deal
Senior Technician, Raine Paul

CHARACTERS

LALLY
DAVE, Lally's boyfriend, Sydney
ELECTRA, New York City
DOSSIE, Lally's grandmother
POP-OP, Lally's grandfather
BELLA, a psychic, New York City
DIEGO, Kansas
PANTHER

MINOR CHARACTERS:

DOCTOR, female, Sydney
ANESTHESIOLOGIST, Sydney
NURSE, Sydney
SURGEON, Sydney
PILOT, into New York City
NEW YORK TAXI DRIVER, female
BELLA'S HUSBAND
BELLA'S DAUGHTER
WAITRESS, at Five Napkin Diner, New York City
MAN, at Electra's apartment
MANAGER, at Duane Reade Pharmacy, New York City
STAFF MEMBER, at Duane Reade Pharmacy
DUANE READ WOMAN
TRAINEE, at Duane Reade Pharmacy
CUSTOMER, at Duane Reade Pharmacy
SHOP ASSISTANT, at shoe shop, New York City
JAKE, NYC date, New York City
MORGAN, retired oceanographer
SUSSAN, Morgan's wife
PILOT, into Kansas
KANSAS TAXI DRIVER, male

DOCTOR, fertility clinic, Kansas
PASTOR, Kansas
MAN WITH BEARD, Kansas church
CAROLINE, aide at Stonebridge retirement community, New Jersey
ELDERLY FAT MAN, Stonebridge resident
MIRIAM, Stonebridge resident
ALEX, Uber driver, Kansas to Miami
CUBAN MAN, Kendall, Miami
SECURITY GUARD, Kendall
MOTHER-IN-LAW of Cuban man
BELLA'S ASSISTANT
HOTEL RECEPTIONIST, Miami
KANYE WEST
COWGIRL, Las Vegas

The original production was performed by five actors, each playing multiple roles.

SETTING

The settings travel from Sydney to New York, New Jersey, Kansas, Miami and Las Vegas. Within these cities are many different locations that come and go quickly. Many are interiors, such as apartments, chemists, cars, shops, bedrooms and doctor's surgeries. Some are exteriors, such as streets, mountains, highways, oceans. It is up to the director and designers how to create this. Good luck!

This play went to press before the end of rehearsals and may differ from the play as performed.

ACT ONE

SCENE ONE

LALLY *and* DAVE *lie in bed.*

LALLY: I know that it's boring to hear about other people's dreams.
DAVE: Correct.
LALLY: But I'll just tell you about this one because it's my most important dream.
DAVE: How can you have a most important dream?
LALLY: The one that shaped your life the most. Please listen. You always tell me about your dreams.
DAVE: When?
LALLY: A few times! I'm always interested to hear about your dreams.
DAVE: Well, that's where we differ.
LALLY: It's not a long dream.
DAVE: Fine, but you can't get angry if I fall asleep and starting having my own dream.
LALLY: Deal. So when I was a child, we lived in Miami and I was really sad because we were about move—to Canberra—I really didn't want I to go. And I really loved panthers—
DAVE: Wait a minute—is this the dream?
LALLY: No, this is background information.
DAVE: That wasn't in the deal. You can't give background information to a dream.
LALLY: If you had've let me tell you it, I'd already be done now.
DAVE: Okay, fine.
LALLY: So I loved panthers—
DAVE: You said that!
LALLY: You're ruining it. If you're not interested I can't tell you.
DAVE: I already told you I wasn't interested!
LALLY: I dreamt that I was at the going-away party at my family's house. But it was only kids. All the grown-ups were out. My cousins were there and my brother. And other kids I guess. And a knock came on

the front door. And through the window on the door, I could see a head. It was the head of a panther. The panther said, 'I'm going to eat you guys'.

I said, 'Wait! Why don't we play hide and seek and you eat the first one of us you catch?'

'Alright,' said the panther. And it began to count to ten. All the kids ran around—looking for somewhere to hide. I could hear the panther counting—one, two three, four, five, six … we were running out of time. And then I remembered—the secret room, behind my parent's ensuite.

DAVE: Was this a real secret room?

LALLY: Not in real life. But in the dream I suddenly remembered it and it was very real. I ran into it—it was just this ordinary, very small room, sort of tan and brown colours. It was the perfect hiding spot from the panther. But my cousins Bobby and Martin were already in there. They told me that I couldn't fit in there with them. They were crouching on the ground. And they kept saying I had to get out. I was so upset with them. But I left, back through the ensuite, and I came out into my parent's bedroom. Now the panther was in the backyard, outside my parent's bedroom, outside the glass sliding door. 'Nine. Ten,' said the panther. And then it told me, 'I'm going to eat you'.

'Wait,' I cried out, as it came inside. 'Can't we just be best friends instead?'

And I couldn't believe it, but it said, 'Yes'. And after that we were best friends. I was so happy. I couldn't believe that I got to be best friends with the panther. We were so happy together. It was like being totally in love I guess. We were in this cocoon, where nothing mattered because we got to be together. But then my last day at school, there was this kid, this scrawny boy named Corey, who was hanging out with the panther. I went up to them. And the boy's father came over and told me, 'The panther is Corey's best friend now'.

'No—no—the panther is my best friend …' I told him.

'No,' said Corey's father. 'Your family is moving to Australia. The panther would have to be in quarantine. You can't be the panther's best friend.'

The panther and I looked into each other's eyes and then he and Corey went to another part of the school. And I sat and sobbed. I wept, with a broken, broken heart.

DAVE: That's your most important dream that's shaped you?

LALLY: I never forgot that panther.

DAVE: I wonder if it's forgotten you?

LALLY: We moved away from Miami to Canberra soon after that. I cried all the way on the plane and at one point deliberately peed in my seat. To see if I'd get away with it. I did. And I've never been back to Miami. Though I think about it all the time.

DAVE: But you're always going to the US.

LALLY: I go to New York all the time to try and do theatre stuff and to New Jersey to see my grandparents. But not Miami.

DAVE: What have you got against Miami?

LALLY: It's the opposite. I don't go back there because it's so special. I was only ever there as a child. So Miami is like childhood to me. I remember my cul-de-sac as being a tropical Smurf Village. And our house had aqua carpet, the same colour as the water at Miami Beach. And white tiles like the sand. I used to pretend to be on a boat floating on that carpet for hours. If I go back there as an adult, it might not be magic anymore. I want to keep it magic. I want to believe that the panther is still there.

DAVE: But he left you for Corey.

LALLY: Only because we moved.

Pause.

DAVE: When I was a kid, Daffy Duck was my very favourite cartoon. He was my role model.

LALLY: You basically are Daffy Duck! You've modelled your whole personality after Daffy Duck!

DAVE *laughs and laughs.*

DAVE: It's true.

They snuggle into each other.

I've thought about it and I think that skin-to-skin contact is actually quite good for humans. It really seems to be raising my serotonin levels.

LALLY: Well, don't just think that you'd get that from anyone whose skin you came into contact with. It's unique.
DAVE: Common human experience.
LALLY: Unique.
DAVE: Regular.
LALLY: You're a jerk.

She kisses his cheek. He smiles.

DAVE: I have to write two whole chapters of my bookity tomorrow. I'm getting close to the actual murder.
LALLY: Exciting! I can read them as you go?
DAVE: Good.
LALLY: If we ever get married can it be in Las Vegas? By Elvis?
DAVE: Okay, time to fall asleep. I'm putting on Alex Jones.

We hear the screaming voice of Alex Jones, the US conspiracy theorist and podcaster, ranting.

Ah, so relaxing.

LALLY *looks up at the audience.*

LALLY: [*to the audience*] Hi, everyone, I'm Lally Katz. I'm a playwright and I wrote this play. I know I should give a disclaimer to stop me from being sued and say that it's work of fiction and none of the characters are based on real people. But to be honest, almost everything in it is true and absolutely every character in it is based on a real person. Now obviously, I'm an actress playing Lally, but that will actually be better in terms of showing emotional truth. Thank you for coming. I really hope you enjoy it.

SCENE TWO

LALLY: [*to the audience*] Now a year later. I'm onstage performing in the theatre downstairs here during a dress rehearsal for a show I wrote about psychics I had dealings with in New York.
[*As psychic*] Your vagina is cursed. Your vagina smells like rotting corpses to all men. Not to women. Only to men. A woman could be in bed wit you all day and not smell a ting. But to all men, your vagina is a cemetery of rotting corpses. Until you pay to remove this curse.

[*To the audience*] After rehearsal I come offstage. But something's wrong. I'm not feeling so good.

SCENE THREE

LALLY: [*to the audience*] By a bin on Oxford Street in Sydney in the middle of the day. I am throwing up in the bin. Dave is holding my hair behind my back.

[*To* DAVE] Sorry. I'm sorry.

DAVE: It's okay. You have nothing to be sorry about.

LALLY: [*to the audience*] A woman walks by and puts her burning cigarette butt in the bin next to my face.

DAVE and LALLY *look at each other and laugh.*

[*To the audience*] In the waiting room of the ultrasound place. I come back out, hobbling because my right side is in so much pain. I sit next to Dave.

[*To* DAVE] There is something on my ovary. He's not sure what it is.

DAVE *thinks about this.*

DAVE: What if you're pregnant?

LALLY: If I am then it would be an ectopic pregnancy. And we haven't really had sex for ages …

[*To the audience*] I realise that he actually seems happy about the thought of my being pregnant.

[*To* DAVE] Do you want to know something gross?

DAVE: What?

LALLY: He said my system is full of poo. He's Chinese and he said, 'You are full of poo-poo'. Imagine if that's what the problem is—just that I'm full of shit.

They laugh.

SCENE FOUR

LALLY: [*to the audience*] In the doctor's office later. I am sitting in front of her desk, crying. She is a nice woman, attractive, Eurasian.

DOCTOR: Do you want me to explain it to your boyfriend?

LALLY *nods, crying.*
LALLY: Yes please. That would be great. Thank you.
[*To the audience*] I go out into the waiting room.
[*To* DAVE] Davey, the doctor wants to explain stuff to you.
DAVE *looks tense. He nods. He comes.*
[*To the audience*] In the doctor's surgery, he sits down, looking tense, looking super polite.
DOCTOR: Hi, how are you going?
DAVE: Good. Thank you.
DOCTOR: There's a very large cyst on the right ovary. Now the fear with a cyst this large that has grown this quickly is that there is a chance it's cancerous. Lally will have to have surgery to have it removed. I've booked her in with a very good gynaecologist. The best one in Sydney, in my opinion. She has an appointment with her on Wednesday. So that's in three days' time. But the other worry with a cyst this large is that it can be very heavy and lead to the ovary twisting inside her.
LALLY: [*to the audience*] I suddenly feel so sad for him. He looks so scared, but he isn't focusing on it, he's focused on being super alert, nodding 'yes' and ready to take in all necessary details. I cry more because I think how he lost his mother and now suddenly we don't know what's going to happen with me and how this sort of thing probably makes him remember that.
DOCTOR: The problem with that is, that the ovary will lose access to blood and will die. Now we want to avoid that happening. So if Lally's pain increases, or if she begins to be in pain when she's just sitting or lying still, then it could mean the ovary is twisting, and if that happens, go straight to emergency. Go to St Vincent's, because that's where the gynaecologist is. Do you have any questions at all?
DAVE: Is there some sort of pain relief she can have in the meantime, because she really is in a lot of pain when it comes on. Or will the pain relief mean that we don't know if it's twisting?
DOCTOR: Absolutely, I'm giving Lally a script. And don't worry, if the ovary begins to twist, the pain relief won't be enough to mask it.
LALLY: And I'll definitely have to postpone my show?
DOCTOR: Oh yes. I'm sorry.
LALLY *nods, crying.*

SCENE FIVE

LALLY: [*to the audience*] Night-time in the Regent's Court Hotel room. I am very sick. My right ovary is twisting. Nothing is working to stop the pain.

> *She is crying, shaking. She sits on an armchair—coiled up, trying to get in a position that stops the pain.* DAVE *is leaning down to her, kneeling.*

[*To* DAVE] Oh, Davey, it hurts. It hurts. Oh, Davey—I don't know, man—

DAVE: It's okay. You're going to be okay. Remember that the pain comes on really strong and then it goes.

LALLY: Davey, it's my fault. It's my fault. Because I thought it might be—because of what the ultrasound guy said about me being full of poo—I thought maybe that was the real reason for the pain—so I had a laxative. They said I could have one—but I shouldn't have—I was okay before that—it's because I had the laxative. I'm sorry.

DAVE: It's not because of that. I think this was going to happen no matter what you did.

LALLY: It's my fault—because I messed around with the psychic in New York. I shouldn't have done that. I can feel her around us.

DAVE: It's not because of the psychic.

LALLY: It's too big a coincidence. She said my vagina was cursed. And now this. But I paid her! I paid off that curse! So why is my ovary twisting?

DAVE: It's just what it is. It has nothing to do with psychics. Besides, they're frauds.

> LALLY *grabs his hand.*

LALLY: Oh, Davey—yikes—oh God, this really hurts—I'm so cold—I don't know, Davey …

DAVE: Okay, now remember that the pain comes on and then it goes. Remember that. Remember that soon the pain is going to be gone.

LALLY: Okay, Davey.

DAVE: And when the pain goes, we're going to go the emergency room. Okay?

LALLY: Okay. Oh God, this is bad, Davey.
DAVE: Remember how it feels when the pain passes. Focus on that.
LALLY: Okay.

SCENE SIX

LALLY: [*to the audience*] The anaesthesiologist, who is funny like a stand-up comedian, wheels me towards surgery.
ANESTHESIOLOGIST: Uh-oh—here comes Nurse Ratched. Don't tell her I changed the port for your IV. She gets very territorial.
LALLY: [*to the audience*] I wave goodbye to Dave.

[*To* DAVE] See you in a couple hours I guess? I'm very high from this morphine. I like it. Hopefully I won't die in surgery.
DAVE. You're going to be fine.
LALLY. I love you, Dave.

[*To the audience*] Even though I'm high, I notice he doesn't respond. He never says it. But I thought I could trick him into it now. I wake up. There are nurses around. They're talking like I can't hear them.

[*To the* NURSES] I've got a tube in my nose.
NURSE: That's right.
LALLY: Um … I seem to have a tube in my nose.
NURSE. Just leave it alone please.
LALLY. Did they have to take my ovary?
NURSE: Wait for the surgeon.
LALLY: [*to the audience*] Time slips. The surgeon comes in.
SURGEON: How are you feeling?
LALLY: Did you have to take my ovary?
SURGEON: I took half of it. If you'd already had children, I would have taken the whole thing.
LALLY: What will happen to the half left over?
SURGEON: It might survive. Or it might wither and die.
LALLY: Is that dangerous?
SURGEON: No.
LALLY: If I want to have children should I do it soon?
SURGEON: Honestly, after this, and you are turning thirty-five, if I were you and I wanted children I would start trying as soon as possible.

SCENE SEVEN

LALLY: [*to the audience*] A couple months later. I stand outside Dave's apartment, ringing the bell.
DAVE: Hello?
LALLY: It's me.
DAVE: I'll buzz you in.

    LALLY *comes in.*

LALLY: I've been living here a year. Can I please have a key?
DAVE: But our system works. Dinner's ready. Protein and vegetables. Pretty bland.
LALLY: I prefer bland. You know I only see food as nutrition.
DAVE: Is that how you see the chocolate that I'm always catching you gobbling up?
LALLY: But it's dark chocolate, Davey! I'm gobbling it for the antioxidants!
DAVE: A likely story. Where did you go today?
LALLY: I walked to Anna's.
DAVE: All the way to Anna's?
LALLY: I like walking.
DAVE: [*as* LALLY] I'm Lally Katz and I'm too whimsical to get my driver's licence.

    They sit down to eat.

I need some last quotes for the book, so I'm going to call the murderer after dinner.
LALLY: Exciting!
DAVE: I need to record myself with before and after thoughts for the bookity.
LALLY: Do you want me to ask you some questions?
DAVE: Yes please.

    He waits.

You can ask.
LALLY: Don't you need to turn your recorder on?

    DAVE *smiles.*

DAVE: It's already on.
LALLY: You sicko! Mine's on too.
DAVE: What are you recording for?
LALLY: In case you say something I want to write a play about.
DAVE: Sicko. Okay, ask me questions about what questions I'm going to ask the murderer.
LALLY: Okay, what's riding on you getting the final part of the story from the murderer?
DAVE: I don't know.
LALLY: Come on, what are the stakes?
DAVE: Everything.
LALLY: The way you see yourself? Your self-esteem?
DAVE: Don't make the questions so girly.
LALLY: But it's true.
DAVE: Okay! Fine. Yes. If I don't get the end of the story then I don't know what I'm going to do in my work and if my work is fucked then my life is fucked, okay?
LALLY: Okay. That's good. Good for you to have that on record.
DAVE: What about you? When are you actually going to write again and not just clean and turn around in figure eights?
LALLY: I write all the time.
DAVE: Sure, if by all the time, you mean never.
LALLY: If you don't want to give me a key to your apartment, maybe we could move to New York and get an apartment together.
DAVE: What am I going to do in New York?
LALLY: Have an adventure with me. Start somewhere new together?
DAVE: No.
LALLY: Well then, maybe we could think about staying here for real and you give me a key and we get married and have a baby.

DAVE flinches.

DAVE: I'm working.

He turns his recorder off.

SCENE EIGHT

LALLY: [*to the audience*] I spend most of each day cleaning the house and talking to my grandparents in New Jersey on the phone.

ACT ONE

[*To* DOSSIE *and* POP-OP] Hi, Dossie and Pop-Op! It's Lally. [*Listens*] I'm good! How are you guys? [*Listens*] Hahaha. I promise I'll come soon, Dossie. Just don't die before I get there. Okay! You either, Pop-Op. [*Listens*] I'll definitely come this year. I promise. [*Listens*] Dave's okay. [*Listens*] No plans for the future yet. [*Listens*] No, he hasn't given me a key yet. [*Listens*] I just ring the bell. No, no I don't live anywhere else. But I'm sure he'll do it when he's ready. Probably once he finishes the book. [*Listens*] You're right, Dossie. I should keep him guessing more. [*Listens*] You're right, Pop-Op. I am living my dreams. Hardly anyone gets to do that. [*Listens*] I'm just sort of working on some upcoming projects ... [*Listens*] No. No new productions. But it means that I'll have time to visit you guys before you die! You better hold out! Love you guys! 'Bye.

[*To the audience*] Then while I clean all the vases I call my parents.

[*To her parents*] I know, I know maybe I need to go back to waitressing. Please stop opening my bank statements, it just worries you. Don't worry, Dave made me give up all my direct debit charities, so at least I won't get fined by the bank anymore for being overdrawn.

SCENE NINE

LALLY: [*to the audience*] Six months later. Dave and I are in the middle of a now-familiar fight.

[*To* DAVE] I thought that maybe now that you've finished your book, that you might have some more time for our relationship ... That you might be more interested ... or attracted to me again.

    DAVE *winces.*

Maybe I'm just freaking out because I'm about to turn thirty-five.
DAVE: Thirty-five isn't a special birthday.
LALLY: It feels so big to me. I feel like I have to work everything out now. Us, my career, having children— Right now I don't have any regrets about our relationship—but how do I know that I won't be forty and you'll marry a twenty-five-year-old and have children with her? Then I would be bitter. Do you understand that? Do you think that's unreasonable?
DAVE: I don't think what you're asking for is unreasonable.
LALLY: **Really?**

DAVE: No, it's perfectly reasonable that you should want those things. That you should want to know where you're at.

LALLY: I just don't want to be an idiot and be thinking I'm in something and I'm not.

DAVE: I understand.

LALLY: [*to the audience*] Dave sits there wincing. Looking sad. His face looks like one sad mask. A tired, sad mask, which he's all of a sudden just put on.

[*To* DAVE] What do you think? What do you think we should do? You never say. Please just say.

DAVE: Maybe you would be happier if we broke up.

LALLY: But do you love me?

DAVE: I guess I do love you. In a manner.

LALLY: Don't you think you'll ever want to get married and have children in your life?

DAVE: Hypothetically I've got nothing against it. Hypothetically. What would you do with children if you had them? Do you reckon you'd get stuff to write about from them?

LALLY: I think so. I think that I would. Like suddenly being open to these whole new worlds of people. Like getting to get to the other parents at the school—you'd have access to all these new characters. You'd be tied to life. I think that would be nice. To be tied to life. You'd like it too I think. If you just gave it a chance. You know you're so fucking brave in your work. You're so fearless. I respect you so much. But in relationships, you're such a coward. All you have to do is say yes. I love you. All you have to do is say yes to me and I promise that it wouldn't be that bad. Please say yes.

DAVE: We're different people, on different paths.

LALLY: No we're not. We're on the same path. You're a writer—I'm a writer. What could be more similar about our paths?

DAVE: You haven't written anything in a year. Have you thought about that? That can't be good.

LALLY: It's because I've been trying to make life work! To make us work!

DAVE: But it's not.

LALLY: But do you actually want to break up? Or do you just think you should—or do you actually want to?

DAVE: Well … I want to.

LALLY: But why?

DAVE: Because … you won't be happy if we stay together.

LALLY: Are you going to date other girls?

DAVE: Well—yes of course.

LALLY: Do you love someone else?

DAVE: No.

LALLY: Do you still love me?

DAVE: Of course I still love you. In a manner.

LALLY: Well, if you love me then why are we breaking up? Why can't we get married and have a baby at the end of the year?

DAVE: Is that your plan?

LALLY: It could be. Can't we just try?

DAVE: I've stated my position.

LALLY: This shouldn't be happening! I had the curse on my vagina removed! You're my soulmate! This should be working!

[*To the audience*] I hug him, crying, in that way when you can't get enough breath and you start gasping. He hugs me back.

[*To* DAVE] But remember—I got you five magnolia trees for the balcony? How can we break up?

DAVE *speaks like a sad robot.*

DAVE: I've stated my position.

He smiles sad. LALLY *waits.*

LALLY: I guess I'll move out soon. Life is so sad sometimes.

[*To the audience*] I take pictures of every room in the apartment. Of the inside, of the cluttered cabinets. Of the dining table where we used to write across from each other. I pack. And I leave.

SCENE TEN

LALLY: [*to the audience*] I am in my new apartment. I am on the line to Telstra. I have been on the phone all morning. Someone's voice comes on.

[*On the phone*] Hello?! Yes. Lally Katz. 0406 749 862. Yes—I had an appointment with Telstra, where from what I can gather, a technician was meant to come and check my phone line and then another technician was meant to install my internet. But only the phone one came. When I joined this plan, they didn't even say that I would need technicians—it was all just meant to come in a package couriered to me. But so anyway, the second technician never came. And I've been without the internet for a month now and I'm sorry, but I work from home and I need my internet put in ASAP. I called last week and was on hold most of the day and we finally organised for it to happen today, but then no-one sent the confirmation text. So I'm assuming that's not happening? [*Listens*] Well, I need it to happen this week. Are you able to make my connection a priority because of Telstra's mistake? [*Listens*] Two to three weeks? I'm sorry, you're really nice and this isn't your fault, you're just one person that I've talked to over the past few days—and every time I get close to something working—the phone cuts out and no-one calls me back—even though they have my number—and then I call back and have to go back into the end of the queue. And it's not your fault, you're just one person I've talked to—but the system is very bad. And I'm sorry I'm going to have to ask to be put through to your manager to make a complaint. It's not about you. You're very nice. But this is a terrible system. And I can't set up my printer without the internet—and I can't start work until I print some things out—and the things I need to print out—a lot of them are from the internet. And it seems like Telstra doesn't want people to get through. So I'm going to have to make a complaint about the system.

The operator can tell LALLY *is crying.*

No, no, it's not your fault. It's the system. It must be hard for you too. You know what, don't worry about it. Don't worry about the internet. Or the phone line. I'm going to go to New York and start my life again. And get a refund from a psychic and hopefully have a baby before it's too late and then I can write again and really be a part of life. No, no I don't need to make a complaint. Thank you.

END OF ACT ONE

ACT TWO

SCENE ONE

A PILOT *speaks.*

PILOT: Good evening, folks. We have begun our descent into New York City. We will be landing at JFK Airport in approximately twenty minutes. I hope you've enjoyed your flight with us. You'll notice how dark it is below, there are many areas of New York still without power after the hurricane. And New York continues to be on high alert for a second hurricane.

LALLY: [*to the audience*] New York City. Speeding through the darkened New York streets in a taxi, I sit in the front seat next to the driver. I feel it's safe because she's a woman. The driver has a long, thin, pale brown ponytail. I notice very soon that she is missing a lot of key teeth. She's overweight, but only loosely. She, like everyone else in this story, is a real person.

NEW YORK TAXI DRIVER: First time to New York?

LALLY: No. I live in Australia. But I was born in New Jersey.

NEW YORK TAXI DRIVER: Jersey—now Jersey got hit even worse than we did.

LALLY: I hope my grandparents are okay. They're in a really nice retirement village.

NEW YORK TAXI DRIVER: A hurricane don't care how ritzy their place is. If it wants to hit, it hits. Where you staying?

LALLY: Airbnb.

NEW YORK TAXI DRIVER: Ain't that illegal in New York now?

LALLY: I think so.

NEW YORK TAXI DRIVER: Well, don't go getting in trouble. After the hurricane it's impossible to get gas. My husband's loser brother is trying, but he's a loser.

LALLY: You're married?

NEW YORK TAXI DRIVER: I got a common-law husband.

LALLY: That's nice.

NEW YORK TAXI DRIVER: Well, it ain't no picnic. He's got seven kids. Ranging from six years old to nineteen. I ain't their birth mother. My husband had 'em with his first wife. But she's a drug addict now and hardly ever wants to see them. Just if they can do something for her. It's real hard on the kids, you know. Especially the middle kids. The older ones have learnt to know better, and the younger ones know me better than they knew her. We keep praying she'll get her life together. She's always asking me for money, but the only salary I got is from driving the cab. My husband's got a disability, so he can't work. And this salary don't go far with seven kids. Plus I'm trying to put some away.

LALLY: Wow. You're an angel.

[*To the audience*] What a great character!

NEW YORK TAXI DRIVER: Well, I got a belief. That helps. Have you ever heard of the lost city of Atlantis?

LALLY: Sure. The myth?

NEW YORK TAXI DRIVER: It's no myth. It was a real city—where everything was perfect. They were real advanced in everything. And then it got taken underwater. Some say that Atlantis was greater than Asia and Africa in size. But I don't think it was really that big. One day and one night Atlantis was taken over by the sea. If it was as big as they said, it would have taken at least a week. But I suppose the sea is powerful though. And Atlantis is still down there under the sea. That's my belief. That soon we'll all be taken back to Atlantis. That's why there's the hurricanes and the floods we been getting so much of lately. So I'm saving up all the money I can, to move my family to Florida, so we'll be the first people taken back there.

LALLY: Miami's in Florida! Will that be taken by the sea?

NEW YORK TAXI DRIVER: Of course. Everybody knows that. Miami'll be the first city to go. It's a shame, because I'd rather move to Orlando. I got a cousin there.

LALLY: [*to the audience*] What she says kind of makes sense to me. Even if she is saving up all her money to take her family to Florida to drown them. I realise that to me, Miami's already under the sea. Perfectly preserved, in another time. It's already an Atlantis. The Miami that I would want to find—my childhood, my family home, my panther— are unreachable in time. And time is just as powerful as the sea.

ACT TWO   17

NEW YORK TAXI DRIVER: My belief is what keeps me going. The world's not like it was. It's people, you know. The weather is acting like the people. Nobody cares about nobody no more. Everyone mindin' their own business, lookin' after their own interests. Didn't used to be like this. And what do we expect? We keep sending satellites up into outer space—every time you do that it breaks up the atmosphere—the ozone—whatever its name is—and the heat gets in. It's gettin' hotter and hotter. And it's because we ain't carin' about other human beings. It makes no sense, you know—you keep building these buildings, takin' away the trees that give the oxygen—what did we think was gonna happen?

She dials her cell phone as she drives and talks.

Atlantis. Atlantis is gonna happen.

Her phone starts to ring.

I can't get no gas because of the hurricane.

She answers her phone call.

Hello? Hello, Jerry—you loser—can you get me some gas or what?

She turns back to LALLY.

This loser can't get me no gas. [*Back to the phone*] Talk to you later then, loser. Call me if you can get me gas.

LALLY: When will it happen? When will you be taken back to Atlantis?

NEW YORK TAXI DRIVER: I don't know the exact date. It changes. Leave me your number. I'm part of a whole network of Atlantis believers. I can let you know when the time comes. We're all gonna head over for it. You can come.

LALLY: Sure.

[*To the audience*] Why not? We arrive at the building. The street is dark and empty. This doesn't look like Greenpoint …

SCENE TWO

LALLY: [*to the audience*] I walk down the hallway of an apartment building. It's concrete. Wide hallways. I pull my heavy suitcase. At the door at the end of the hallway, a woman's head pokes out. Electra. She's of Puerto Rican decent, but speaks with a thick Brooklyn accent. She's got long, long, curly hair—which I am soon to find out is a hairpiece.

[*To* ELECTRA] Electra?

ELECTRA: Oh, you're so pretty!

LALLY: Really? These clothes are really bad. I know that they're bad. I was trying to look like a businesswoman for the flight—but these clothes are really bad—

ELECTRA: No, you look great.

ELECTRA *hugs her.*

LALLY: You look great too.

ELECTRA: No, I gotta lose some weight. This ain't the real me. In three months' time—after I been working out—that will be the real me. So let me show you the apartment.

LALLY: [*to the audience*] I go into the apartment. It's nice, but very dirty. There are self-help/empowerment/spirituality books everywhere.

ELECTRA: I'm trying to clean up—does it look okay to you?

LALLY: Oh, yeah—sure. It's fine.

ELECTRA: Do you mind if I hang out for a bit—my friend is coming to pick me up soon, but she's always late, and I got to wait for her so she can take me to my other apartment, 'cause I can't ride my bike with all the stuff I gotta take. Plus in this weather I can't ride a bike at all. I mean I like riding around the neighbourhood, you know, I do that most days. But not when there's been the flooding. But, you know, the weather's not the main thing that stresses me. Every couple weeks moving—so I can keep making ends meet with this Airbnb thing—that's what it's like—very stressful. Now listen, I know what you want in New York City. You want to get laid.

LALLY: What? How do you know that?

ELECTRA: It's New York. You come here on your own. You're looking for fun. Also I know what else you want—you want weed. And I can get it for you anytime. I can get it for you tonight even if you want it tonight.

LALLY: Oh, thanks—but I can't handle it—I get very paranoid.

ELECTRA: That's okay—it's okay to be conservative. You just be yourself—don't apologise.

LALLY: No, I'm not conservative—it's just that I try to dress like a businesswoman when I fly so that they might upgrade me.

ACT TWO 19

ELECTRA: You don't have to explain nothing to me—just be yourself.
LALLY: [*to the audience*] I give up, unhappily, into the role of the conservative businesswoman.
ELECTRA: Now you just use anything of mine. You can walk on my treadmill here in the corner—actually it's more of a StairMaster—but I'm always calling it the wrong thing. And you wear my clothes—anything you want.
LALLY: That's so nice of you.
ELECTRA: And there's a towel in the bathroom for you, but I got some more in this closet. Here's one.

She pulls a towel out of the closet. It is small, faded, crumpled, full of holes. And looks unwashed.

LALLY: Thanks.
ELECTRA: You wanna wash anything there's communal laundry at the other end of the hall—all you need is quarters. Hey, can I ask you a big favour?
LALLY: Uh, sure.
ELECTRA: You mind if my dog stays here tonight?
LALLY: [*to the audience*] I notice a very small dog asleep in a ball. Oh—really?
ELECTRA: She won't need go to the bathroom or nothing. It's just I've gotta spit tonight—
LALLY: Like rap?
ELECTRA: Haha! That's funny! I didn't pick you to know a word like that! Conservative type like you. I gotta spit tonight. Or I'm gonna lose it, you know. And I can't take her nowhere with me. I tried sneaking her in, in my sweater once, but, you know—she's a quiet dog—not that night. That night she was barking like a bitch man and we got kicked out of the club. I can't take that chance tonight with this crazy weather, you know. I need to spit. I got to. Tonight.
LALLY: Okay, sure you can leave the dog. Should I take her outside for a walk or anything?
ELECTRA: No, you don't gotta do anything like that tonight. Just take it easy. And by the way, you can see around here, I got a lot of self-empowerment books—I highly recommend. I mean that's what I'm doin'. I'm listening for the signs. I'm looking out. Something dope is gonna happen for me soon.

SCENE THREE

Grandparents POP-OP *and* DOSSIE *sit in their apartment in the retirement village. Their phone rings very loudly. Neither of them hear it. Finally* DOSSIE *looks up.*

DOSSIE: Martin, I think someone's calling.
POP-OP: You think so?
DOSSIE: Yes. It could be Ricky.
POP-OP: Okay then, I'll answer it. But if it's Miriam I'm going to pretend the power has cut out.
DOSSIE: It won't be Miriam. She has bridge today.
POP-OP: Bridge will be cancelled.

He makes his way over very slowly and answers the phone.

Hello? Hello? Oh, hello—Lally! [*He turns to* DOSSIE.] It's Lally!
DOSSIE: Lally!
POP-OP: [*into the phone*] Dossie's going to get on the other line. Where are you? [*Listens*] New York?! [*He turns to* DOSSIE.] She's in New York!
DOSSIE: New York?

She gets on the phone.

You came! You got through the storm?
POP-OP: You sure are full of surprises! When can you come to New Jersey? [*Listens*] Pardon?
DOSSIE: She said she'll come tomorrow.
POP-OP: Wonderful!
DOSSIE: We kept up our end of the bargain. We're still alive. And you've kept up yours. You've made it back to see us one more time.

SCENE FOUR

LALLY: [*to the audience*] But before I visit my grandparents there's somewhere else I have to go first. I stand outside Bella's psychic shopfront. I ring the bell. Bella's husband opens the door. He is wearing his white singlet, with food stains. Inside, it is heavily heated. Some of the heat wafts out onto me and some of the cold slips in

ACT TWO

through their door. Bella's husband is chewing a toothpick, above his jutted-out bottom lip.

LALLY: [*to* BELLA'S HUSBAND] Hi, is Bella in?
BELLA'S HUSBAND: She read for you before?
LALLY: Yes. But not for a while.
BELLA'S HUSBAND: Do you got an appointment to see her?
LALLY: No—is she busy?
BELLA'S HUSBAND: No.

BELLA'S HUSBAND *goes back inside.*

LALLY: [*to the audience*] A little bit of time passes, and then Bella comes out, dragging her heavy body, wearing a singlet top, her arms flapping out the sides.

BELLA *moves slowly. Looks tired. Like she can't be bothered. She gives a weak, tired smile.*

[*To* BELLA] How are you, Bella?
BELLA: It's been a long day.
LALLY: Crazy weather, huh? Did you know that the storm was coming?
BELLA: I had no idea. None.
LALLY: Do you remember me?
BELLA: You been here before?
LALLY: Yes, about a year ago.
BELLA: Like I said, it's been a long day. If you been here before you should have my card. How come you didn't call for an appointment?
LALLY: I thought that was just a formality.
BELLA: You should have called—I could have, you know, been out. I wasn't. But I coulda been.
LALLY: I wanted to see you about something specific. You remember how you took a curse off of me before?

Slight pause.

You took a curse off my vagina, remember?
BELLA: Uh-huh …
LALLY: Well, it helped for a while. And then it stopped working. So I want a refund.
BELLA: No refunds. Besides you said a year ago? That's way outside of warrantee.
LALLY: You remove a curse and it should be for life.

BELLA: Says who? Curses come, curses go. A doctor don't give you a flu shot and guarantee it'll work for life.
LALLY: Well, you should have told me it would expire. Because now it's over. I lost my soulmate.
BELLA: You can't lose your soulmate. If you lost him, he weren't your soulmate.
LALLY: Well, last time you told me he was.
BELLA: You gotta stop holding onto last time. Last time this, last time that. Enough of the past. I tell the future. And what I can do for you is remove the new curse that has set in.
LALLY: Well, I hope you're going to do it free of charge.
BELLA: I can't work for free. I got a family. Besides with these secondary curses, they're tough. What I can see, is some very jealous, negative energy has got attached to your aura. It looks to me like it's a jealous wizard who's got a grudge on you from a past life. Wizards are tough. It's gonna be a lot of work for me. So it ain't gonna be cheap.
LALLY: How much?
BELLA: How much did I charge you last time?
LALLY: Three hundred.
BELLA: It's gonna be a lot more than that because this is something big.
LALLY: More?
BELLA: At least two thousand.
LALLY: Two thousand? Are you kidding me? No way.
BELLA: I don't know if you can afford not to do it. 'Cause it's only gonna get worse.
LALLY: No.

She turns to walk out.

BELLA: And you ain't getting any younger.

LALLY turns back around.

Just sayin'. I don't know if you're plannin' on having kids et cetera. And the soulmate findin' game gets pretty vicious around your age.
LALLY: Is there any bargaining room—at all?
BELLA: I'm giving you bargaining room—I'm not even charging you my price. I'm omitting my fee because I know you.
LALLY: I'll think about it.

ACT TWO

BELLA: Well, don't think about it too much—because from what I see around you, it's really a big situation.
LALLY: There's no way you could go down to one thousand?
BELLA: Let me put it to ya this way, the lowest I can go is eighteen hundred. And that's stretchin' it, because this is gonna be nine candles at two hundred dollars a candle. And I gotta take the candles and light 'em all the way up in the mountains.
LALLY: What mountains?
BELLA: Never mind. But what I can tell you is that the window for mountain work is closing—because the weather's gettin' bad—and I gotta book my assistant and order the materials.
LALLY: [*to the audience*] Just then, the door opens and Bella's thin, lank, energyless teenage daughter comes in.
BELLA'S DAUGHTER: Mom?
BELLA: You know you gotta knock when I got a client.
BELLA'S DAUGHTER: Dad said for me to tell you the 'Real Housewives of Atlanta' is comin' on soon.
BELLA: Okay. Good girl.

BELLA'S DAUGHTER *stands in the doorway.*

Tell Dad I'll be there in a sec.
BELLA'S DAUGHTER: Can I go downtown for a little while?
BELLA: No. Stay here.
BELLA'S DAUGHTER: Please?
BELLA: Your brother is gonna come from uptown later. That's enough uptown, downtown in one day. Now let me finish up with my client.
BELLA'S DAUGHTER: Please?
BELLA: Go back there with your father.

BELLA'S DAUGHTER *glumly leaves.* BELLA *turns back to* LALLY.

Now the sooner you give me the money, the sooner we can do this. Before the weather comes in.
LALLY: I'll think about it.

LALLY *goes to leave.*

BELLA: Fifteen hundred. But you're ripping me off.
LALLY: Deal. I'll put it on my credit card.

LALLY *takes out her credit card.*

BELLA: I don't take credit. You know that.
LALLY: I'm low on cash right now.
BELLA: So buy some American Express gift cards from Duane Reade. And put them on your credit card.
LALLY: How come you take those but not credit card?
BELLA: I don't got a machine. Them, I can use like cash.
LALLY: Okay, I'll come back soon.
BELLA: Don't take too long. The future is not lookin' good.

    LALLY *leaves.*

SCENE FIVE

LALLY: [*to the audience*] First I go to write in a New York bar. But because I'm by myself I feel embarrassed and just go to this weird burger bar called Five Napkin that's like a fast food joint that sells cocktails. The cocktails are terrible. And they go so fast.

  [*To a* WAITRESS] Could I get another martini please?

WAITRESS: Of course, honey.

LALLY: [*to the audience*] But instead of writing, I look through my phone. Through Instagram for pictures of Dave. I follow the names of women who have liked or commented on his photos to find out if they are now his girlfriend. Who's this? Jenny Vincent? Why is she liking so many of his posts? I'm going to her page. What? He's liking her posts too!

    LALLY*'s phone rings.*

[*To the audience*] Dave?!

    She looks at the phone. It's not him.

[*On the phone*] Dossie? Hi, Pop-Op. I know—I'm so sorry—I got held up with some business here. Yes. Some meetings. Yes. Very productive. I'll come tomorrow. Love you. 'Bye.

WAITRESS: Here you go, honey.

    The WAITRESS *hands* LALLY *another drink.*

LALLY: Thanks. I'll take a glass of tequila too please.

[*To the audience*] That night I sleep with a guy who has facial prosopagnosia. He tells me that he can't tell if I'm beautiful or not because he can't compare my face to anyone else's. The next night I drink. The night after I sleep with a guy with a backpack, studying to be a brain scientist. He tells me that the brain is always seeking out pathways of rewards. A few days later I sleep with a cop who's related to Sylvester Stallone. He has his eyebrows. But none of it helps.

A week later. I'm not feeling so great. Electra still hasn't come to get her dog. I'm a mixture of drunk and hungover. My jetlag won't let me sleep at night and I hate being awake with a broken heart at four a.m., so I just drink until I pass out.

>LALLY *drinks Gatorade and takes ibuprofen. Her phone rings.*

[*To the audience*] Sorry, Dossie. Sorry, Pop-Op. I lie in bed, following the rabbit holes of Facebook. I have a big cut on my leg. Like a strawberry sort of graze. It really hurts. I don't quite know how I got it. I think I must have been running for a taxi or a train and I fell. I get up, my head aching—blasting me. I go into Electra's medicine cabinet in the bathroom. It's all just half-used cans of hairspray, Revlon moisturisers, pharmacy beauty products, half-covered in leftover shower steam and the dust that sticks to it. I don't find any antiseptic stuff. But I take a picture.

Wounded and sad, I go back to my computer. I look at Dave's face. He used to say when I was injured or sick that I took it emotionally and that I would 'moop'. He would look at me and say, 'What are you mooping about?' and I would look back at him and say in a sad, sorry voice, with tears in my eyes, 'Moo-oop'.

I look at his face.

[*To* DAVE] Moop. Moooop.

[*To the audience*] I go to send him a message. But can't think of what to write except 'I hurt my leg'. I send it. I wait for a response. With bated breath I wait. I can see he is on Facebook. He is active. No response. I write 'Moop'. No response. I wait. No response. And then I cry.

> *A knock on the door.* LALLY *is startled by this. She goes silently over to the door. She listens to hear if it will happen again. And then* ELECTRA*'s voice calls out:*

ELECTRA: Hey, you home? It's just me—Electra.

>LALLY *opens the door.*

LALLY: Electra! Thank God it's you—I thought it might have been a murderer.

 ELECTRA *laughs.*

ELECTRA: Just me—I came to get my bike.
LALLY: And the dog?
ELECTRA: Not yet … You been walking her?
LALLY: Yeah.
ELECTRA: Oh, thank God!
LALLY: But, Electra—I don't really have the time to walk a dog regularly right now.
ELECTRA: Why, what you doin'?
LALLY: Well, nothing—but I have to go to New Jersey soon to see my grandparents—
ELECTRA: Jersey ain't far. You can get there in a day and back.
LALLY: I'm not really used to having a dog around.
ELECTRA: It's very good for you. Pets really change the energy of a home. You know what, let's you and me take her outside down there to the common area down there. Be good for the other residents to see us together anyway, so they believe you're my friend and not get suspicious about all this Airbnb bullshit. It ain't allowed in this building. So many stupid rules. Good for them to see us together, just hangin'.

 LALLY *drags herself up.*

Hey now, there you are! Why you been hiding that body? Damn!
LALLY: Thanks … I'm so hungover I feel like I'm going to die.

 LALLY *takes a drink from her Gatorade bottle.* ELECTRA *laughs and pulls out her own Gatorade bottle.*

ELECTRA: Now you're living my life! 'Livin' La Vida Loca'. Come on.
LALLY: [*to the audience*] I don't want to hang out with Electra. Or her dog. This Airbnb isn't ideal. But it seems easier to go with at this point. We walk down the hallway. A big, fat, old Latino man is sitting out the front of his apartment. He looks us up and down.
MAN: You know I love it.
LALLY: [*to the audience*] We stand outside in the pouring rain and the wind. The dog runs around, peeing everywhere. My head is throbbing, but the rain kind of helps.

ACT TWO

ELECTRA: So you don't got a boyfriend?
LALLY: No. He broke up with me.
ELECTRA: What for?
LALLY: He didn't want to have kids with me.
ELECTRA: I can't believe you just said that. I am going through exactly the same thing.
LALLY: Really?
ELECTRA: All the time. I don't know what happened to all the men. I can't even think about it 'cause it makes me wanna cry. The choice to have a baby, to be a mama, it's being taken away from me and I ain't even got a say in it. Because the men aren't men. I'm stuck in this situation—that so many good women I know—dope women I love—are stuck in. We are living in a time like we never had before. And you and me, we are in trouble because of that time. It ain't you. It ain't me. We're two women—two artists—spitting out in the world—and the time ain't ready for us. The only thing that comforts me, is I got someone real special from my past who is gonna come back for me.
LALLY: I probably should go inside. I'm worried about the rain infecting this cut on my leg.
ELECTRA: It'll clean it out for you. So this was a long time ago. Very soon after my dad's death. And I was real upset, you know. My world in a very quick time got turned upside down. I was fighting to keep it together, you know. And just after my dad died, I'm waiting for my boyfriend to pick me up. And he's late, yo. So already I'm feeling bad, right? And then he comes and he's got this bitch in the car with him. This bitch I never seen before. And he knows my dad's just died and he knows that and he's got this strange bitch—this ho in the car with him—when he should be there for me. And I ask him, 'Who dis?' And he laughs like it's funny. And I just say to him—I tell him, 'You're not even one piece of shit. You're fucking dog slop.' And I walk away and I can feel the tears coming. I can feel the pain of my dad's death—of knowing that I got to be the one to take care of my family now—the pain of being betrayed by this motherfucker that I trusted and I can feel it I'm gonna cry—but then I don't cry. I start spitting. Right there on the street—I start rapping—it's coming out of me—I can't stop it—I'm just about to turn down a side street—I can't stop it—I'm spitting—spitting—and then I look up and there's

this guy in a car. And his eyes meet mine. And he smiles. He calls out to me, 'Hey—hey!'

But I don't want this—I'm upset, you know, about my boyfriend—about my dad—and I turn down the side street and keep walking away. Walking fast now—still spitting. And he follows me in his car. Nice car. 'Hey stop! Stop!' He calls out to me.

And I look at his car and he's different, you know—he's not a hood nigga. He's artsy, you know. And he's got personalised licence plates. He gets out of the car saying he drove all the way from Chicago. And the licence plates say 'Kanye'. You know who that is?

LALLY: Of course—I love Kanye.

ELECTRA: See, now everybody, even conservative types like you, know who he is—but he ain't nobody back then. He starts telling me he wants to produce me. He looks at my face and he asks me if I got my scars in a car crash. And he shows me he's got the same scars. Also from a car crash. It's destiny he tells me. And he asks me what rappers I like. I tell him Jay Z and he tells me, 'I work with that nigga'. And he thought that was gonna be what won me—he thought that was gonna be what clinched the deal—but what he didn't know is that's what made me turn the other way. See that nigga who I was with before—the one who just come by with that bitch in the car—he collaborated with Jay Z too and I didn't want nothing more to do with him. So I start walking away again. And he's following me. And he ask me, 'What do you want to be when you're twenty-five?'

And I just looked at him and said, 'Still alive'. And he started laughing when I said that. And you listen to his songs now—you listen to 'Welcome to the Jungle' with Jay Z and you hear that line. And I started to run away from him and he's chasing me. But I just keep telling him, 'Now is not our time. Now is not our time.' Because you got to understand my dad had just died—my boyfriend had just hurt me by coming to get me with this bitch—and I wasn't ready—I ran away from him, he chased me and I screamed at people to help me and I screamed to him, 'Now is not our time!'

LALLY: Why didn't you go with him?

ELECTRA: You think I don't ask myself that every single day?

LALLY: Maybe it wouldn't have been a good thing.

ELECTRA: I missed my chance. On everything.
LALLY: Maybe your time will still come?
ELECTRA: He'll be back for me. No doubt. And you listen to his music and you'll hear it in the words. And you'll know who he's really singing about. And you look up his film *Runaway* on YouTube. You watch that. And you will see our story.
LALLY: [*to the audience*] After Electra leaves I go back to the Five Napkin Diner and drink more bad cocktails. And I decide, I don't want to miss my chance like Electra missed hers.

SCENE SIX

Duane Reade Pharmacy. The MANAGER *and a* STAFF MEMBER *are fussing around the cut-out of a woman.*

MANAGER: She was working this morning.
STAFF MEMBER: I don't know why she's being so fussy today.
MANAGER: Try the reset button again.

>*All of a sudden, the cut-out of the* DUANE READE WOMAN *lights up. She suddenly has all the features and colouring of a woman.*

DUANE READE WOMAN: Hi, welcome to Duane Reade Pharmacy. I'm Valarie. Have you joined our Duane Reade Rewards Points? If not, sign up for it today, it's free and takes less than five minutes. You will be eligible for points and discounts on a huge range of products.
STAFF MEMBER: She's back!
DUANE READE WOMAN: Have you checked out our promotion in aisle twenty-two?

>LALLY *enters.*

LALLY: Excuse me, which section are your American Express gift cards in?
MANAGER: Aisle eight, by the cash register.
LALLY: Thank you.

>[*To the audience*] I take the American Express gift cards from the stand. And I walk over to the cash register.

TRAINEE: [*to the* STAFF MEMBER] What am I meant to do with these?
STAFF MEMBER: Has she got any ID?

LALLY: Yes here's my passport.

The STAFF MEMBER *looks at it and then looks at the cards.*

STAFF MEMBER: I need the manager to authorise them.

LALLY: [*to the audience*] She calls the manager. He arrives.

MANAGER: How come you're getting so many?

LALLY: Because I need to pay someone fifteen hundred dollars who doesn't take credit card and I can't really afford to make the payment in cash right now. So I figured I could buy these cards and pay for them on credit card.

MANAGER: Who are you paying?

LALLY: [*to the audience*] I realise that there's a lot of other customers who have gathered around to listen.

[*To the* MANAGER] Um … A psychic who removed a curse on me. But now I have a new curse. And this time she's charging a lot more.

MANAGER: I know the lady you're talking about. And she's banned from this store. She's a crook. She's a dangerous person.

The MANAGER *shakes his head. The* STAFF MEMBER *looks at* LALLY.

STAFF MEMBER: What you seeing that lady for? She playing you.

LALLY: That may be so, but I really need to pay off the curse.

CUSTOMER: You know there are people starving on the streets, sleeping in the rain—no shelter from the weather—and you giving her your money? I pray for you.

MANAGER: You want to believe, you look to God.

STAFF MEMBER: I be praying for your soul.

CUSTOMER: My daughter sees a good psychiatrist, that actually might be cheaper.

MANAGER: You need to look inside yourself and find belief. All the answers are in there. You can't find answers in other people. Don't you know that by now?

LALLY: Maybe not all the answers—but don't you get some answers from other people?

MANAGER: I'm not selling you the gift cards.

LALLY: Thank you. Thank you for your help. You're very wise.

[*To the audience*] I walk out ashamed. And go to the ATM. Damn. I'm gonna run out of money.

SCENE SEVEN

LALLY: [*to the audience*] I stand inside, Bella's daughter is wearing her pyjamas.
LALLY: Sorry, I think it might be kind of late. Is your mother still working?
    BELLA'S DAUGHTER *shrugs.*
BELLA'S DAUGHTER: She don't really have exact hours.
LALLY: Could you tell her that there's a customer here who wants to make a payment?
    BELLA'S DAUGHTER *goes out.* LALLY *looks at the moons and suns hanging up.* BELLA'S DAUGHTER *comes back in.*
BELLA'S DAUGHTER: You have to wait a little while. Until there's a commercial break.
LALLY: I don't mind waiting.
    BELLA'S DAUGHTER *looks at* LALLY *awkwardly.*
BELLA'S DAUGHTER: You can sit down if you want.
LALLY: Can I interview you?
    LALLY *takes out her recorder.*
BELLA'S DAUGHTER: No. That's not allowed.
LALLY: I'm a writer. I need new characters. I think you could be good.
BELLA'S DAUGHTER: Well, don't never tell my mom.
LALLY: Okay. So do you have the gift too?
BELLA'S DAUGHTER: What?
LALLY: The gift. The psychic ability?
BELLA'S DAUGHTER: Oh yeah, I guess.
LALLY: What year are you in at school?
BELLA'S DAUGHTER: I don't know.
LALLY: High school?
BELLA'S DAUGHTER: I'm homeschooled.
LALLY: Oh—like in being a psychic?
BELLA'S DAUGHTER: I guess.
LALLY: That must be a burden. Having the gift sometimes.
BELLA'S DAUGHTER: Just the way I grown up.
LALLY: Do you have other friends who are psychics?
BELLA'S DAUGHTER: Some.

LALLY: All girls?
BELLA'S DAUGHTER: Yeah. I'm not allowed to have boyfriends. Not till I get married.
LALLY: Maybe that'll save you a lot of heartache.
BELLA'S DAUGHTER: It's my mom's choice. And my dad's. Nobody cares what I want. It's the same for all my friends too. But they don't want their freedom like I do.
LALLY: Can you and all your friends see what each other are thinking?
BELLA'S DAUGHTER: I guess. Mostly I'm usually good at finding things that people lose. Specially silver. Not gold. But I know where silver is most of the time when people lose it.
LALLY: I don't really have much silver.
BELLA'S DAUGHTER: Your earrings are gold.
LALLY: Yeah.
BELLA'S DAUGHTER: What's that in 'em? A diamond?
LALLY: Yeah. They were given to me by my neighbour.
BELLA'S DAUGHTER: Your neighbour gave you earrings with diamonds in 'em?
LALLY: She's an old lady. Hungarian. I wrote a play about her.
BELLA'S DAUGHTER: Don't lose those earrings, 'cause if you do, I can't find 'em. Only silver. But my main job is cleaning my mom's crystals.
LALLY: Oh, like when the moon is full? You reprogram them?
BELLA'S DAUGHTER: My mom usually just tells me to clean 'em with Windex.
LALLY: With Windex?
BELLA'S DAUGHTER: Uh-huh. Keeps 'em fresh and clear.

> BELLA *comes in, dragging her heavy body, wearing a singlet top, her arms flapping out the sides.* LALLY *quickly puts her recorder away.* BELLA *looks at her* DAUGHTER, *seemingly not having heard anything that they have been saying. She moves her head, as in, 'Go to the other room'.* BELLA'S DAUGHTER *doesn't look at* LALLY *and heads out of the psychic shopfront into the out-of-sight living area behind.*

BELLA: What's the point in you taking my card when you never call? You just show up?
LALLY: Sorry. I brought the money.
BELLA: You made the smart choice.

ACT TWO   33

LALLY: Can I talk you down to thirteen hundred?
BELLA: What did I tell you it would be?
LALLY: Fifteen hundred.
BELLA: No. I can't go any lower. I told you—didn't I—about the weather. It's very dangerous work for me. Nature is comin'.
LALLY: Okay. Fifteen hundred.

> LALLY *hands her the money.*

How will I know when you've done it?
BELLA: Oh, don't worry. You'll know.

SCENE EIGHT

LALLY: [*to the audience*] Jenny Vincent has again posted on Dave's timeline. This time a picture of the two of them in the coffee shop near his house. I email my friend in Sydney and ask her to introduce me to a friend of her boyfriend's who works in finance in New York and asked about me after seeing one of my plays. If Dave is going to be happy with someone else, then I will too!

On the way to meet Jake, I suddenly realise that I can't wear the rain boots that I'm wearing on a date with a man in finance. So I go into a shoe shop.

> *In the shoe shop. trying on shoes.*

[*To a* SHOP ASSISTANT] Do you think these boots sort of go with anything, like they're sort of casual, but also could be classy?
SHOP ASSISTANT: Yes.
LALLY: So they don't look like they're too dressy for a date, like I'm trying too hard, but they also look classy, like not sloppy and too casual?
SHOP ASSISTANT: Definitely.
LALLY: How much are they?
SHOP ASSISTANT: They're on sale for four hundred dollars.
LALLY: Great …

> [*To the audience*] We meet up in a thriving bar in the East Village. He's handsome! He's in finance. This is my new life! I feel sorry for Dave because it will be a big blow losing me to someone like this.

JAKE: I loved your show. I was really glad Sean brought me.
LALLY: Oh, thanks!

JAKE: It was such an amazing night. I was so excited. I mean it was unbelievable.

    LALLY *is getting super excited.*

LALLY: Wow …
JAKE: Just incredible. I'll tell you what blew me away.
LALLY: What?
JAKE: That Rose Byrne was there.
LALLY: Oh.
JAKE: Do you actually know her?
LALLY: Only a little bit.
JAKE: But she was actually at your show.
LALLY: She's really great about supporting Australian work.
JAKE: I just couldn't believe that she was there. She is someone I always fantasised about meeting. And, oh my God—in real life—she's even more beautiful. It's unbelievable really. Like wow. But I didn't work up the nerve to go over and introduce myself. Damn it.
LALLY: Oh, that's a shame …
JAKE: Does she have a boyfriend?
LALLY: Yeah. They have a baby.
JAKE: Oh, okay. Darn. Oh, well. It was still so exciting just seeing her at your show.
LALLY: [*to the audience*] I'm suddenly so embarrassed in front of myself that I bought these boots.

SCENE NINE

LALLY: [*to the audience*] I go back from the date to Five Napkin Diner and get drunk. I get drunk for another week and a half. I have lots of missed calls from Dossie and Pop-Op. Shit. I can't believe I haven't been to see them. I realise that I've been in New York for two weeks and all I've done is look at Dave's social media, get drunk and walk Electra's dog. Electra comes by that night. Not to get her dog. She's smoking a joint and we're watching 'Doctor Phil'.
ELECTRA: Smoke some pot. Mama. It'll relax you.
LALLY: I get paranoid.
ELECTRA: What's wrong with that?

    She hands LALLY *the joint.*

ACT TWO

LALLY: [*to the audience*] And suddenly smoking pot doesn't seem like that bad an idea.

> LALLY *lifts the joint to her mouth.*
>
> *They are sitting on the couch, facing each other. Looking intensely into each other.*

ELECTRA: Man, the shit that I can see. It just make me more lonely, you know, mama? Because it set me apart from people, yo?

LALLY: I understand. I understand more than you think.

> [*To the audience*] Electra looks at me, partly with suspicion, partly with hope.

ELECTRA: Tell me how you understand, mama.

> LALLY *is so stoned. In between sentences, she closes her eyes—partly with the emotion of what she's saying—which feels very real to her—partly with the zinging of the pot.*

LALLY: I hear things. I feel things. But if I tell people about it they pull away. I'm always in contact with the other world—with the hidden world. But they keep me from being really part of life.

> ELECTRA'*s eyes fill with tears. She puts her hand on her heart and nods.*

ELECTRA: How you know that? How you know that's exactly what I feel? I never talked to no-one who got me like you do.

LALLY: Me too. Me too with you.

ELECTRA: I was so alone, man. I was so lonely.

LALLY: Me too. I was so lonely. I kept trying to find people. Like my boyfriend, but he couldn't do it.

ELECTRA: Fuck him, man. Flick him off your pussy, mama. Take your hand and flick him off your pussy. Copy me now. Flick him off your pussy. He don't deserve to be nothing to your pussy.

> ELECTRA *demonstrates how to flick him off her pussy,* LALLY *copies.*

LALLY: Flick him off my pussy!

ELECTRA: That's right, mama! Flick him off there!

LALLY: I'm flicking him off my pussy!

ELECTRA: Flick him!

> LALLY *flicks him.*

That's better, huh?

LALLY: Yeah. Thank God I've found you. All those times alone. Eating meals alone. I'm always alone.

ELECTRA: Me too. Me too. But not anymore.

LALLY: Thank God. Thank God we found each other.

ELECTRA: You and me, we gonna be business partners. You can stay in any a' my Airbnb places for a discount if you book early. We gonna sort this shit out. You bring in your Australian friends—we gonna be in business together. You up for this, mama? You ready to be my partner?

LALLY: Yeah! Totally! I really need a job. I've almost run out of money. And I have no writing prospects.

ELECTRA: I am crying all the time because I'm forty-two and I'm not a mama.

LALLY: Me too. That's why I'm lonely too. We should have children. But instead we're alone. What are we gonna do? We're running out of time.

ELECTRA: You can get your eggs frozen real cheap now in Kansas. They got a deal going to try and help 'em out of the financial hole they're in. I keep seeing commercials about it. If I get more Airbnb business—damn, that's the first thing I'm gonna do.

LALLY: I'm gonna do that too. That's a great idea.

ELECTRA takes LALLY over to the bathroom mirror.

ELECTRA: You are a beautiful woman. You should be attracting value. Look at you.

LALLY: I get really paranoid looking at myself when I'm stoned. I see all the ugly stuff.

ELECTRA: Bullshit. You look and you look good. Because you got real assets.

LALLY: You look beautiful.

LALLY looks at ELECTRA in the mirror.

ELECTRA: No, I don't want to look at me now, because this shit that's goin' on with my skin—it ain't right.

LALLY: You have beautiful skin.

ELECTRA: Don't play with me. I got these spots. But you is gonna be my inspiration.

ACT TWO

LALLY: You know what I use?
ELECTRA: What?
LALLY: Jojoba oil. I put it all over my face every day. It gets in my eyes and makes the world look muddly, but I think it really helps with wrinkles.
ELECTRA: Okay, I'm gonna try that shit.
LALLY: I don't think it's good for your eyes—I have to warn you.
ELECTRA: I could not give a fuck about that.

She lights up another joint.

And I know that everything—everything—even the furniture is alive. It's all alive.
LALLY: I know. I've always felt that too. Do you hear voices?
ELECTRA: All the time. They be tellin' me to do some bad shit.
LALLY: I used to get that. So I'd have to sleep with music on.
ELECTRA: Why you think I keep the TV on?
LALLY: But you don't hear voices telling you to do bad stuff to me, do you?
ELECTRA: I want to tell you no. But they is always there.
LALLY: I don't feel so good, Electra. I think I have to go to sleep. I'm so glad we found each other. You never know who your soulmates are going to be.
ELECTRA: I know, mama. We're gonna be business partners.
LALLY: [*to the audience*] I lay, fully clothed, and pass out in Electra's bed. I wake up and she's pressed against me. Running her hand over my ass and breasts. Panicked, I close my eyes and pretend to be asleep. I keep waking up all night, on the edge of the bed, with Electra still pressed against me, feeling me up. I don't feel strong enough to have a confrontation with her. And I'm a little scared about her hearing those voices. And I don't know where I'd go when it's so late, raining so hard, and I'm so out of it. So I just keep pretending to be asleep. But, Jesus, I'm thirsty, and my head hurts. I'm in my old house in Miami. I dream there's someone knocking on the sliding glass door.

LALLY wakes up with a gasp.

And then I remember. I wait until six a.m. And then I quietly pack my stuff. I take pictures of everything in her house for writing reference later. I whisper from the doorway:

[*To* ELECTRA] Electra, sorry, I wish I could be your soulmate. But I have to go.

SCENE TEN

LALLY: [*to the audience*] On the train to New Jersey. I look out through the window at the land my parents were born, grew up in, married in. Where my brother and I were born. The trees outside though are ripped down. The ground is messy. What happened, I think to myself? Oh, that's right. Nature is coming.

SCENE ELEVEN

LALLY: [*to the audience*] In the dining room of the old people's home. I am sitting with my grandparents, Dossie and Pop-Op.
[*To her grandparents*] Now I'm sorry it's taken me so long to get here.
DOSSIE: We know you have a very busy life. We're just so glad you've made it. I didn't think I would get to see you again.
LALLY: I told you. A deal's a deal.
POP-OP: Tell us more about the playwriting business.
LALLY: Honestly, it's a little slow right now.
POP-OP: But it's great that you're following your dreams. I did have a few notes on the last script that you sent me.
LALLY: Oh, really?
POP-OP: Just a few little tips that I think might help it get produced. How are you earning a living right now?
LALLY: Earning a living is kind of a strong way of putting it …
DOSSIE: And you really broke up with Dave?
LALLY: Well, we broke up. That's actually something I wanted to talk to you guys about. I was hoping that—I wanted to ask if—

    MORGAN *and* SUSSAN *enter.*

POP-OP: Oh—look who it is! Lally, this is Morgan, one of the world's leading oceanographers. Who just happens to live here now. And this is Sussan, his wife.
LALLY: Wow! Congratulations. To you. Both. [*She turns back to her grandparents.*] What I wanted to ask was—
DOSSIE: [*to* MORGAN & SUSSAN] Won't you join us?
SUSSAN: Sure. We'd love to.

ACT TWO

MORGAN *and* SUSSAN *sit down.*

POP-OP: Our granddaughter is a writer. You should tell her about some of your adventures being a top oceanographer, Morgan.

MORGAN: You're being too generous, Martin. As usual.

POP-OP *is holding a microphone attached to headphones so that he can hear.*

POP-OP: You're being too modest, Morgan. Morgan was one of the oceanographers chosen by Princeton for their research. You were part of that team for years, Morgan. And he was also one of the government's core oceanographers. You are one of the world's leading oceanographers, Morgan.

MORGAN: Now I'm just a retired grandfather.

MORGAN *and* SUSSAN *laugh.* DOSSIE *turns to* POP-OP, *speaking loudly.*

DOSSIE: What did he say?

POP-OP: Pardon?

DOSSIE: What did he say?

POP-OP: He said he's just a retired grandfather now.

DOSSIE *laughs.*

DOSSIE: He's too modest.

POP-OP: That's what I told him.

LALLY: Dossie, there's something I need to ask you and Pop-Op—

POP-OP: Tell us, Morgan. Did you see all this disaster coming? Did you know climate change was coming, back in your day?

MORGAN: We've known about it since the early seventies. With physics we could predict it. But what we couldn't predict was what people's reactions would be. We never could have predicted that it would become such a political issue. And what we also couldn't predict was China. Was how much China's rise would affect it.

LALLY: Oh, yeah. China. Dossie—

MORGAN: And it's fair enough. We had our turn. We can't stop them. We just didn't see it coming.

POP-OP: How high will the water rise?

MORGAN: We don't know yet. It depends how long it takes the ice to melt.

LALLY *turns to him.*

LALLY: Will it definitely melt?
MORGAN: Yes. It will definitely melt.
LALLY: Do you know what cities will be underwater?
MORGAN: If there's not drastic procedures undertaken immediately, I would say a lot of cities will be underwater.
LALLY: Will Miami really be one of them?
MORGAN: Miami will certainly be one of them. New York will go. Venice of course. Any low-lying island. And the coastlines of many continents—they will be gone too. Geography will be very different.
LALLY: [*to the audience*] That crazy taxi driver was right.

[*To* MORGAN] Is there any way to stop it?
MORGAN: People would have to change significantly. I don't think there's the drive or the want to.
LALLY: So there will be all these new Atlantises.
MORGAN: Yes. That's a nice way to look at it.
POP-OP: You might want to go visit Miami and see your old haunts before it's too late. You had your childhood there.
LALLY: No. I want to leave it how it is. In my memory.
POP-OP: Memories aren't all that dependable. Especially at our age!

DOSSIE *speaks to* LALLY.

DOSSIE: Speaking of memories. I thought maybe we could look at photographs today. I have some of your family, when you were all young, that I thought you might like to take with you.
LALLY: Sure—
DOSSIE: Do you remember how we used to do the treasure hunts at Miami Beach? We'd do the treasure maps and you and Mikey would find a treasure chest of candy buried under the sand. And then your father would get angry about me sneaking candy to you.
LALLY: Yes. I loved those treasure hunts. Dossie. I hate to ask you this. But I'm in a bind. Since I lost the ovary and Dave and I broke up, I need to freeze my eggs. In order for our line to continue. I wouldn't ask you, except that it concerns all of us. I don't have any money. And it's usually twenty thousand dollars to freeze your eggs. But it's only fifteen thousand in Kansas. It's a really good deal. And it might not last long. Could you guys help me?

DOSSIE: Is that why you came?
LALLY: No.
DOSSIE: You'll have to ask your grandfather about money. But I do have this for you.

She hands her a sweater covered in red hearts and red butterflies.

I thought you might like to have this sweater. To remember me by.
LALLY: It's beautiful. You should keep it.

DOSSIE *laughs.*

DOSSIE: You don't like it.
LALLY: No, I like it. Thank you.

LALLY *takes the sweater.*

Pop-Op ...
POP-OP: I heard.
LALLY: You never hear anything.
POP-OP: Why don't you wait a little while and see if you meet someone?
LALLY: I don't have a little while. [*To* MORGAN *and* SUSSAN] I'm sorry ...
MORGAN: We should probably be moving along anyway.
POP-OP: Don't go. This discussion is over.
LALLY: Really? What about our family line?
POP-OP: You're behaving very rudely and unlike you.
LALLY: I better go. I'm sorry. Sorry.

[*To the audience*] And I go.

SCENE TWELVE

LALLY: [*to the audience*] Out the airplane window, I watch America pass beneath me. Even from the sky, it looks battered.
PILOT: Ladies and gentlemen, please take your seats, we are now beginning our descent into Kansas. As you can see below there has not been rain here in a very long time. And that is not going to change today. The weather in Kansas is hot and dry. Be careful of sun exposure. I wouldn't want anything to ruin your time in Kansas.

SCENE THIRTEEN

LALLY: [*to the audience*] I am sitting in the back of the taxi.

KANSAS TAXI DRIVER: You wanna hear something funny?

LALLY: Sure.

KANSAS TAXI DRIVER: Did you ever think to yourself, today is the tomorrow I worried about yesterday?

LALLY: What do you mean?

KANSAS TAXI DRIVER: Well, tomorrow is gonna come no matter what—so why worry about it?

LALLY: That doesn't make sense. Because we can determine what kind of tomorrow it's going to be by worrying.

KANSAS TAXI DRIVER: Nah. You just gotta make it through the day with a smile on your lips and a fifth on your hip. I try and make people laugh to forget their troubles. Because no matter what, they're gonna be here. So where you heading?

LALLY: Honestly, I'm going to the fertility clinic to try and freeze my eggs.

KANSAS TAXI DRIVER: Well, these are interesting times. Can't say that they aren't.

LALLY: It sure is hot and dry here.

[*To the audience*] Can this place really be the best environment for keeping my eggs frozen?

KANSAS TAXI DRIVER: Yup. Drought. I lost my farm. I lost my house. Keep smiling.

LALLY: Oh. I'm so sorry.

KANSAS TAXI DRIVER: Oh, don't you worry about it, my dear. I got shot in the ass, didn't I? What you gonna do? So now I drive around, workin' for somebody else. Drivin' people around. And have fun. This country's a joke. You know, I'm a simple man and you make things simple, sometimes it works better. That's not how the country's run. But I can't get upset about it. 'Cause I can't change it.

LALLY: [*looking out the window*] Oh—what's that?

KANSAS TAXI DRIVER: It's tumbleweed. Nature's way of saying hi.

LALLY: Hi, Nature.

SCENE FOURTEEN

At a fertility clinic.

LALLY: So I can pay in instalments on credit card? I just don't have the cash upfront. But it's not like the whole procedure happens at once, is it?

DOCTOR: We could take your money. But honestly your egg count is so low, I don't think it would be worth trying to freeze them. Your best bet is to just try and get pregnant as quickly as possible. Do you have a partner?

LALLY: No.

DOCTOR: Well, you could consider artificial insemination.

LALLY: Yes.

DOCTOR: It's what a lot of women do.

LALLY: So I could do that. And get pregnant?

DOCTOR: Possibly.

LALLY: But it would just be me. On my own?

DOCTOR: Well, I can't predict your future.

LALLY: Can I think about it and come back in?

DOCTOR: Of course. It's a process.

SCENE FIFTEEN

LALLY: [*to the audience*] I walk along the highway. Massive pick-up trucks pass me. There's no sidewalk. But I want to walk. I walk past the closed-down shops. Past the boarded-up houses. Deserted cars. I follow the highway past dried-out farms. The only people I see on the street are the homeless. I pass one man who doesn't look up at me as we pass each other on the highway. I walk by a dried-up creek bed and I hear a voice whisper from behind a bush …

VOICE: Ma'am …

LALLY: [*to the audience*] And it sounds like a voice wanting help. But I'm scared of the help they might want. So I run down the highway. I'm thirsty. And the pilot was right about the sun. Tumbleweed passes and I take a picture of it, to remember Nature's way of saying hi. I keep walking. The highway is deserted. There's nothing. There's no-one. If I had a baby, would that mean I wasn't alone? Or would I just be bringing someone into the world to be lonely with me? Shouldn't it be easier to just make life? Why does it have to be such a big question?

I come to a church. A church in the middle of nowhere. But there's cars parked in the parking lot.

I walk in. It's like a Hillsong sort of thing, only older and not popular. A big sign saying 'Vineyard'.

> *Beautiful music plays. Friendly faces. A band is playing. The* PASTOR, *who is waiting to go onstage, sees her and smiles. Very welcoming. He beckons her in with his arm.* LALLY *sits in the pews with the other churchgoers.*

The pastor comes onto the church stage. He speaks about God and the economy.

PASTOR: I know people have been hurting because of the drought, because of the factories closing, because of the bankers. But you must come back here to God, because that's the only island from this pain.

LALLY: [*to the audience*] He says he knows people have been feeling lonely.

PASTOR: Lonely. Have been feeling isolated. Have been feeling angry. Have been feeling loss. But that is the devil. The only way to escape the devil is to come back to the Lord.

LALLY: [*to the audience*] A tear comes into my eyes, because like America, I have been feeling lonely, feeling lost. As the pastor talks, another man comes over and sits with me. He has a beard. The pastor's talking begins to turn into singing. It's beautiful.

MAN WITH BEARD: Welcome. We love when newcomers come. Where are you from?

LALLY: Australia.

MAN WITH BEARD: No kidding! Australia. Wow, how about that. I've always wanted to go to Australia.

LALLY: It's really not that far. Only a day away.

MAN WITH BEARD: What brought you to Kansas?

LALLY: I wanted to have a baby. I want to not be alone. I want to find love. Can you help me?

MAN WITH BEARD: Only God can give the gift of love. And only God can take away the pain of love. Come to God. And all love will be yours.

LALLY: Okay. I'll do it. I'll come to God.

MAN WITH BEARD: How did you get here?

LALLY: I walked here.

MAN WITH BEARD: You walked here?

LALLY: Oh yeah, I walk everywhere. Even places where there are no sidewalks.
MAN WITH BEARD: You walked here all the way from Australia?
LALLY: Uh—
MAN WITH BEARD: I think you're an angel. I think you're an angel that's been sent here to show us that we're on the right path. Shirley, Debbie, I want you to come meet someone.
LALLY: [*to the audience*] Two women, one middle-aged, one in her late thirties, come over.
MAN WITH BEARD: What's your name?
LALLY: Lally.
MAN WITH BEARD: Lally.

He turns to them.

Lally walked here from Australia. She's an angel. I want you to take her up to the front and pray for her. Pray for her to find love. Lally, is that alright with you?
LALLY: Yes please. I'd like that very much.

The music plays. The PASTOR *sings.*

[*To the audience*] Debbie and Shirley lead me up to the front. Everyone is standing up now, praying for each other. They raise my hands above my head. They put their hands on my arms. They pray for me. They cry. I cry too.

SCENE SIXTEEN

LALLY: [*to the audience*] Walking back along the highway, I hold my own hand. It's getting dark. But I'm not scared. I come into the city. It's night. If I can just keep this feeling. If I can just be enough. Be with my own heart. And just see what life does.

And then, at the lights, a handsome Latino guy with a Texan accent says:
DIEGO: Excuse me, I'm looking for a bar.
LALLY: [*to the audience*] Interval.

Interval occurs here.

END OF ACT TWO

ACT THREE

SCENE ONE

LALLY: [*to the audience*] And then, at the lights, a handsome Latino guy with a Texan accent says:

DIEGO: Excuse me, I'm looking for a bar.

LALLY: Which one?

DIEGO: Is there one you like? What's a good club?

LALLY: I hate nightclubs.

DIEGO: Nah, you just never go to them, so you think you hate them. Come with me. Just for a little while.

LALLY: How old are you?

DIEGO: Thirty.

LALLY: I don't believe you.

DIEGO: You wanna see my licence?

LALLY: Yes.

He shows her his licence.

Huh. You are.

DIEGO: Everyone always thinks I'm young.

LALLY: You're lucky.

DIEGO: Nah. When you're a man you want to command respect. That's why I'm thinking of growing a beard.

LALLY: Gross.

DIEGO: Beards are in fashion. So am I old enough for you?

LALLY: I don't like nightclubs. I can't dance.

DIEGO: Come just for one drink.

LALLY: I'll tell you what. I'll walk somewhere with you. But I'm not coming in. I just like walking.

DIEGO: Fine with me.

LALLY: [*to the audience*] I feel so comfortable with this guy. I don't know why. But it just feels easy. We arrive at a nightclub.

DIEGO: Come in for one drink.

LALLY: I hate nightclubs.

ACT THREE

[*To the audience*] Inside the club music pumps and it's dark. Diego goes to get me a margarita. It tastes like toothpaste. I look around and realise I'm the second oldest person in here. The oldest person is a big white guy in his fifties, sort of dancing on his own, but as though it's with the whole room.

DIEGO: How's your drink?

LALLY: Good.

DIEGO: You want to taste mine?

LALLY: What is it?

DIEGO: Vodka and Red Bull.

LALLY: That's okay.

DIEGO: Taste it.

LALLY: [*to the audience*] I have a sip. It tastes like medicine.

[*To* DIEGO] It's good.

LALLY's phone rings.

DIEGO: Who's calling you so late? You got a boyfriend?

LALLY: No. It's my grandfather.

She puts her phone away.

Do you live here?

DIEGO: Dallas. But I wasn't born in America.

LALLY: Where were you born?

DIEGO: Mexico. My dad got this bright idea that he didn't ever want me to grow up and join the American army, so he smuggled my mom back into Mexico before she gave birth.

LALLY: So are you a citizen here?

DIEGO: Nope.

LALLY: [*sarcastic*] Wow, that must not be fun now.

DIEGO: Yeah. My dad fucked me over. And then he left. My mom became a Jehovah's Witness. I used to go door knocking. I was really good at it. It's the only religion that takes science into account. That's why it's the best one.

LALLY: Are you still a Jehovah's Witness?

DIEGO: No. It doesn't work with my lifestyle. But I still believe in the religion. That's why I know I'm going to hell.

LALLY: You're not going to hell.

DIEGO: I wish you were right. Only way I can be saved is if Atlantis takes me. Only way any of us can be saved. You know about Atlantis?
LALLY: Yes. I do.
DIEGO: We all gotta pray for it to come. Wanna dance?
LALLY: I'm a terrible dancer.

> DIEGO *leads her onto the dance floor and begins to grind his pelvis against hers.*

[*To the audience*] He doesn't seem to notice how awkward I am.

> DIEGO *offers her more of his drink. She reluctantly has a sip. He leans in and kisses her. She kisses him back.*

[*To* DIEGO] Are you chewing gum?

> *He nods.*

DIEGO: You want a piece?
LALLY: No thanks.

[*To the audience*] I look around at all the young faces.

[*To* DIEGO] I should get going.
DIEGO: What, really?
LALLY: Yeah.
DIEGO: Well, I'm going too.
LALLY: You can't come with me.
DIEGO: Of course not. I'll just walk you for a bit. It's only fair after you walked me here.
LALLY: Okay, but you're not coming in.

[*To the audience*] We get to my hotel.

DIEGO: I really have to pee.
LALLY: You can't pee in my room. Only in the lobby.
DIEGO: No problem.
LALLY: [*to the audience*] There's no bathroom in the lobby.

[*To* DIEGO] Okay, you can pee in my room, but you're not staying.
DIEGO: Totally.
LALLY: You're not a serial killer, are you?
DIEGO: [*with a laugh*] No.
LALLY: What do you do?
DIEGO: I work for myself, but through a company that sells a miracle health supplement called Kyani.

ACT THREE

LALLY: What does it do?

DIEGO: Cures cancer, gets rid of fat, just makes you live longer. You name it. I've been selling this product for three years and it's really starting to pay off. I've got a car through them back in Dallas and everything.

LALLY: How did you start working for them?

DIEGO: A friend signed me up. And then I've returned the favour by signing up my family and friends. And whenever they sell something, I get a percentage. It's the American dream. To be your own boss. I got flown here for this big conference they're doing because my sales are so good. You want to try some?

LALLY: No thanks. It sounds like a cult.

DIEGO: All sales sound like a cult. But seriously, I believe in the product. Just try a little.

LALLY: Are you sure you're not a serial killer?

[*To the audience*] We go into my room. He comes out of the bathroom.

DIEGO: Thanks. I'll see you soon?

LALLY: [*to the audience*] But wait ... Is this my prayer to God answered? Well, now that you're here ...

She kisses him.

[*To the audience*] All my reservations are gone. He takes my shirt off and my bra off.

DIEGO: Nice.

LALLY: [*to the audience*] He takes his shirt off.

LALLY *laughs.*

[*To* DIEGO] Whoa!

DIEGO: What?

LALLY: Look at you. You've got a twelve pack.

DIEGO: I work out. And I take Kyani.

LALLY: [*to the audience*] He guides me over to the bed, taking both of our clothes off.

[*To* DIEGO] Have you got a condom?

DIEGO: No, but I'm ready to have children anyway.

LALLY: Really?

DIEGO: Sure.

Afterwards. LALLY *and* DIEGO *lie entwined in each other's arms.* DIEGO *is absentmindedly massaging her shoulder.*

LALLY: How do your fingers know exactly where the pain is?
DIEGO: I had a Ritalin earlier.
LALLY: Do you have ADD?
DIEGO: No. I just like the extra focus. It helps me to read people. But I just get you. It's so crazy. That we both happened to be walking right there. At right that time. If you were there one minute sooner, or one minute later, I wouldn't have met you.

I feel like you haven't been held in a while. Am I right?
LALLY: Yeah. How can you tell that?
DIEGO: The Ritalin. You ready to go again?
LALLY: Yeah.

[*To the audience*] We have sex again. And looking out the window, I realise it's the afternoon. We've been in bed for about fourteen hours. And I know in my core, that I've met my soulmate. I wake up. Very, very sore from all the sex we've been having.

SCENE TWO

LALLY *sits across from the fertility* DOCTOR.

LALLY: I met someone. And I think we're going to have children. So I won't need to continue.
DOCTOR: Well, that was fast.
LALLY: Yes.
DOCTOR: Congratulations.
LALLY: Thank you. We've been having a lot of sex. So I think it may happen soon. I can't believe it. That everything is just going to be resolved so quickly. I feel so lucky. Like I put a wish—a longing out into the universe—a prayer actually—and now it's been answered. All we do is have sex! Although I think my vagina may be injured from too much sex.
DOCTOR: Injured?
LALLY: It really hurts to walk. To pee. I mean it really hurts. And itches. I feel like there's all these little cuts in it. But I'm so happy.
DOCTOR: Would you like me to take a look?

ACT THREE

LALLY: Sure, that would be great. Thank you.

The DOCTOR *looks at her vagina.*

DOCTOR: I can tell you right now, you have herpes.

LALLY: What?

DOCTOR: You can do a test, but that is textbook herpes.

LALLY *gasps.*

LALLY: I have herpes ...

DOCTOR: It is a very common STD. There is very effective treatment available.

LALLY: You can cure it?

DOCTOR: No. Herpes is for life.

LALLY: For life ...

SCENE THREE

LALLY: [*to the audience*] Diego opens his hotel room door.

DIEGO: Good to see you.

LALLY: [*to the audience*] He sits in front of his laptop. He finishes showing me a cut-together video about the illuminati on YouTube.

DIEGO: You want a Ritalin?

LALLY: No thanks.

DIEGO *pops one in his own mouth, never looking away from the screen.*

DIEGO: I like to mix them with Kyani for the ultimate results.

He looks at the screen.

Beyoncé, Rihanna, Madonna, all illuminati. See how they all keep making the pyramid sign?

LALLY: I don't think so. The triangle sign is just a popular shape to make and that's why the conspiracy theorists chose it.

DIEGO: You know Rihanna's tattoos contain secret codes about how to kill off most of the world's population?

LALLY: But then who's going to buy her albums?

DIEGO: She won't need the sales. She'll just take all our left-behind wealth.

LALLY: I think you might be mistaking Rihanna for the Nazis ...

> DIEGO *considers this.*

DIEGO: Okay. Here's a scenario for you. Hitler's not dead. He's tied up in this room. You have a gun and a knife. Do you kill him?

LALLY: It might be a bit intense killing him. Maybe I'd just ask him some questions.

DIEGO: Questions? A master manipulator like Hitler who controlled half the world? He'd get you to untie him.

LALLY: I wouldn't untie him.

DIEGO: He'd sell you to his way of thinking. You wouldn't even know it was happening.

LALLY: I don't think so.

DIEGO: I do. The best punishment would be to get a Jewish woman to torture him.

LALLY: That could be me. I could be that Jewish woman. Or half Jew.

DIEGO: But you'd get carried away and it would get too sexual.

LALLY: I would not have sex with Hitler!

> DIEGO *shrugs.*

DIEGO: Anyway, did you come here to have sex? 'Cause I gotta get back to work soon.

LALLY: I came to tell you something.

DIEGO: What?

LALLY: I … I think you gave me herpes.

> DIEGO *is flustered, upset.*

DIEGO: I don't have herpes.

LALLY: Most people who have it don't know they have it.

DIEGO: I get STD tests all the time.

LALLY: Apparently they don't test for herpes unless you request it. Here's a herpes fact sheet. It's very helpful.

> *She goes to hand it to him.*

DIEGO: I don't have it. So you have herpes?

LALLY: Yeah. I have it. Number one. Apparently that's the good kind of herpes, so that's good news.

DIEGO: So you have herpes and you're accusing me of giving you herpes?

LALLY: Not accusing. Just letting you know.

DIEGO: It sounds like you're the one who has it and you're giving it around. You saw my cock—it's smooth and clean!

ACT THREE

LALLY: You could have been invisibly viral shedding.
DIEGO: Gross!
LALLY: I'm not trying to upset you.
DIEGO: Well, how did you think I was gonna react?
LALLY: I thought you might admit that you have it and take responsibility.
DIEGO: I don't have it and exactly what kind of responsibility would I take anyway?
LALLY: Well, I kind of think, you broke it, so you bought it.
DIEGO: What?
LALLY: My vagina. You broke it, you bought it. I think we should get married. In Las Vegas.
DIEGO: What? Are you joking?
LALLY: I'm thirty-five years old. And now, I've got herpes. You need citizenship. We get married. It's perfect.
DIEGO: What makes you think I'm not a citizen?
LALLY: You told me the other night.
DIEGO: Damn Ritalin. All these diseases are just created by the government anyway. They've got a cure for all of them. But they're getting paid by the drug companies.
LALLY: I don't think that's true.
DIEGO: You don't think it's in the illuminati's interest to keep people sick and paying for medicine?
LALLY: I don't think the illuminati invented herpes. But I think you gave it to me.
DIEGO: I gotta get to the airport. My flight back to Dallas is in two hours. I can't really take this in now. It's been a big week with the conference. You want to take some Kyani for it? It might help.
LALLY: No thanks.
DIEGO: All you'd have to do is see if you like it and then maybe sell some to three other people. Like your brother maybe? Or some of your close female friends.
LALLY: No. I don't think so.
DIEGO: Your choice. But it's a good product. I have to go.
LALLY: I could come. I could come with you to Dallas.
DIEGO: I'm sorry—but I'm not looking for a relationship.
LALLY: No. No. You have to be with me. Who else will love me now? With herpes?

DIEGO: I gotta go. Get yourself together.

    LALLY *takes a deep breath.*

LALLY: At least we'll always share herpes.

DIEGO: Yeah, but I don't have it.

    LALLY*'s phone rings. She takes it out.*

  You can answer it.

LALLY: It's just my grandfather. I'll call him back.

  [*To the audience*] Pretending I'm writing a text message I take photos of Diego, his suitcase and his hotel room.

SCENE FOUR

LALLY: [*to the audience*] I sit at Stonebridge with my grandfather. He is barely sitting up. A hired nursing aide, Caroline, is there to help.

CAROLINE: Granddad's very happy that you're here.

LALLY: I'm sorry it took me so long, Pop-Op.

POP-OP: We were very worried about you. You know, I was thinking. About your situation. You have so much to be proud of. You're living your dreams. No-one gets to do that. The only mistake you made was spending so much time with Dave. It was clear he wasn't going to commit in the beginning. A man shouldn't be careless with a woman's time. It's the worst thing he can do.

LALLY: Yeah.

POP-OP: That was a mistake.

LALLY: [*to the audience*] I wheel Pop-Op in his wheelchair down the hallway of Stonebridge. It is a different kind of feeling, to be so in control of another human being. Of my grandfather. We pass other elderly residents, either in chairs, or on canes, or leaning on the hallway railings. When each one of them sees someone with youth passing, their faces light up. And they wave as though to passengers in a launching ship.

  I wheel Pop-Op around the brunch buffet in the dining room.

POP-OP: I'll take the eggs, but no muffin and no ham.

LALLY: [*to the audience*] We fill up his plate. We sit across from each other, eating. I'm eating. Pop-Op only occasionally has a little bite. The two old elderly men dining next to us are both quite fat. Their plates are piled high and they are eating and eating.

ACT THREE

POP-OP: Food is repulsive to me now. I'm repulsed by the look of it. And it all tastes like sawdust. As soon as I take a bite, I want to spit it out.

He spits out a little bit of it onto his plate.

Dossie had the right idea. Getting out quickly.
LALLY: The only time in her life that she was punctual.

POP-OP *laughs.*

POP-OP: It's true.
LALLY: Are you afraid of dying?
POP-OP: No. I just don't want it to take a long time.
LALLY: Do you think there's anything after death?
POP-OP: No. No I don't.
LALLY: Will you miss yourself?
POP-OP: Good question. But who will be this 'I' that will miss 'me'?
LALLY: Good question. Where are Dossie's ashes?
POP-OP: No, I don't want any rashers.
LALLY: No, where are Dossie's ashes?

He holds his microphone up to her.

Where are Dossie's ashes?
POP-OP: Oh, Rick has them. Because he's the one most likely to make it to Bar Harbor. And he'll scatter them over the water there.
LALLY: What will happen with your ashes?
POP-OP: Oh, I've left my body to science. I've got a very interesting tumour on my brain that a med student might be able to learn from. I hope it's of some use to him.
LALLY: Or to her.
POP-OP: I hope so.
LALLY: I'm going to miss you.

[*To the audience*] I realise that one of the fat elderly men is pointing at me and smiling. I smile back at him.
ELDERLY FAT MAN: You should wear that sweater back here on Valentine's Day.

He points to the white sweater with red butterflies that LALLY*'s wearing.*

LALLY: Thank you. It was my grandmother's sweater.
ELDERLY FAT MAN: It's perfect for Valentine's Day.

He smiles at POP-OP.

I'm jealous of you, Martin.

POP-OP *smiles politely, but doesn't really hear.*

LALLY: [*to the audience*] I wheel Pop-Op back through the hallway. We go up a slight slope.

POP-OP: Oh, you got good momentum there.

LALLY: [*to the audience*] Just then, my grandfather looks up.

POP-OP: Oh, no. She's coming.

LALLY: [*to the audience*] Down the hall, Miriam, a wiry, little lady, about a hundred years old, but strong and full of energy, is zooming towards us on a walking frame.

POP-OP: Oh, she's coming right for us.

MIRIAM *waves. She strides quicker with her walking frame.* POP-OP *looks disgusted.*

MIRIAM: Hello, Martin. So nice to see you.

POP-OP *says nothing, just fumes.* MIRIAM *turns to* LALLY.

Well, look who it is. I thought it was you. But I couldn't believe it! Your grandfather must be thrilled! I'm thrilled. Oh, look at you!

She pinches LALLY*'s cheek.*

Tell me. How are you? Tell me everything. How long are you here for?

LALLY: I'm leaving back for New York tomorrow.

MIRIAM: Oh no—were you here for the big storm?

LALLY: I just missed it.

MIRIAM: And did you bring your boyfriend with you?

LALLY: No. We've broken up.

MIRIAM: Oh, I'm so sorry. What a terrible shame. You poor thing.

LALLY *smiles.*

Well, sometimes these things work out for the best. But it never makes it easier at the time.

LALLY *nods.*

But you're a great girl. You'll be okay.

LALLY: Thank you, Miriam.

[*To the audience*] She stands there holding my hand. Pop-Op throws his hands up in the air in fury. I'm not quite sure how to make our exit. But at the same time, it does feel nice, kind of healing, to be standing there, holding one-hundred-year-old Miriam's hand.

 CAROLINE *helps* LALLY *take* POP-OP *inside.*

[*To* POP-OP] Did you want to have a rest, Pop-Op?

POP-OP: Maybe that's a good idea.

LALLY: [*to the audience*] I sit at the table and try to write. But I'm lost in the story. There's a photo album on the table, with pictures of our treasure hunt in Miami. And the map. Pop-Op's oxygen machine bubbles softly, soothingly, comfortingly, against the wall. An hour passes and I hear him coughing.

POP-OP: Is Lally still here?

LALLY: I'm here, Pop-Op.

[*To the audience*] Pop-Op watches the big football game, wearing his headphones, while I try on Dossie's jackets. I'm trying on a light denim jacket with gentle and beautiful embroidery.

 CAROLINE, *the aide, comes in.*

CAROLINE: Oh, that fits you very well!

LALLY: You think so? But maybe I've got too many things now?

CAROLINE: Why do you say that? Your grandmother's clothes fit you very well! Where else will they go? Don't leave any behind!

 LALLY *shows the jacket to her grandfather, he is watching the football, with his special headphones on.*

LALLY: What do you think of this one?

POP-OP: Oh, stunning! It's absolutely stunning on you! Dossie's clothes are a perfect fit for you.

CAROLINE: I told you. Don't leave any. Take them all.

LALLY: [*to the audience*] The football game is playing silently on the television. Pop-Op is wearing his earphones and microphone. He looks like a newborn baby. With his bald head supported up against the back of the chair.

[*To* POP-OP] It feels like Dossie is still here.

POP-OP: I know. I talk to her all the time. Especially at night. Sometimes I hear her talk back. Is that crazy?

LALLY: No.

POP-OP: Maybe it would make a good play.

LALLY: Maybe.

POP-OP: She passed along so quickly. She had just finished making a batch of fudge. For Margery because her son was coming to visit. And I was cleaning up after her in the kitchen. And then she was lying on the floor. She thought she'd fallen. She didn't know it was a massive stroke. It all happened quickly after that. When they asked her if she wanted to be on an IV, she said out of the one half of her mouth, 'I'd rather a chocolate bar'. She kept her sense of humour and her personality right to the end. She was her. Right to the end. It was a privilege to spend these years with her. But now my use in this world is finished.

LALLY: [*to the audience*] Pop-Op's eyes look the softest I've ever seen them.

POP-OP: I sang her the 'September Song' as she died. I don't know if she heard it. People say though that they can hear things—as they're passing. Do you know it?

LALLY: No.

POP-OP: It's an old man singing to a young woman. He's got a lot of nerve—to ask for her youth. What more arrogant thing could an old man ask for than a young woman's youth? She doesn't marry him. Thank goodness. But in the end he's happy for her and he spins on his wooden leg at her wedding.

LALLY: Will you sing it for me? Can I record it?

POP-OP: Well, once a ham, always a ham I guess.

> *He coughs. And then sings several verses of 'September Song' (Kurt Weill/Maxwell Anderson).*
>
> *When he's finished,* LALLY *claps.*

LALLY: Thank you.

POP-OP: You better go soon. It's getting dark out.

LALLY: I'll miss you both for the rest of my life. Knowing how much you both loved me. You've been such a gift in my life.

POP-OP: Sweetie. You were our first grandchild. We're so proud of you. I just wish you could have had a relationship like mine and Dossie's. I would have loved that for you.

ACT THREE 59

LALLY: [*to the audience*] Crying like I did when leaving Dave, but I fight it back. I hug my grandfather. Hold him like a frail baby.
[*To* POP-OP] I hope I see you again.
POP-OP: I don't know where that might be.
LALLY: [*to the audience*] I go out into the New Jersey night. I take the Miami treasure map. The wind whips the rain. It's time to go home.

SCENE FIVE

LALLY: [*to the audience*] At the airport, waiting for my flight to Miami.
ANNOUNCEMENT: Ladies and gentlemen, unfortunately all flights to Miami have been cancelled. Unfortunately, at this time, it is not safe to fly into Miami due to the super hurricane headed directly en route to it. We apologise for any inconvenience, but it is no longer safe to fly into Miami.
LALLY: [*to the audience*] Shit. I have to get to Miami. I can't drive. Shit. I know. I'll call an Uber. A young Uber driver named Alex, in a Prius, picks me up.
ALEX: You want me to drive eighteen straight hours to get to Miami when it's about to be hit by the most massive hurricane in history?
LALLY: Yes.
ALEX: Nah. Sorry.
LALLY: I'll give you fifteen hundred dollars.
ALEX: Alright then. What address should I put in my GPS?
LALLY: I need to get to my old house.
ALEX: You think you can direct me to it?
LALLY: It's in the suburb of Kendall.
ALEX: Got anything more specific?
LALLY: I'll get the address from my mum.

    She calls her mum.

[*On the phone*] Hi, Mum, what's our old address in Miami? [*Listens*] Okay. Great. Got it. [*Listens*] Um … No reason. I'm going there. [*Listens*] No, it's okay, because I'm in a car. [*Listens*] Mum, please stop opening my bank statements. I'm not going to be all alone in the world and broke. I promise. I know you're scared for me. But I promise. I'm going to be safe. This is the best thing I could possibly be doing. I love you.

[*To the audience*] I feel a little bad that my parents are worried ... But I'm en route with Alex.

ALEX: You know, it's funny, you picked the right Uber driver. I'm actually from Miami originally. I've only been living in New York about six months, so it's actually real good for me to get back there and see my family.

LALLY: [*to the audience*] Alex speeds down the New Jersey Turnpike, as he tells me about his life. He was born in the Dominican Republic, but had lived in Miami all his life. He had been in six serious car accidents and totalled six cars.

ALEX: You know, they did a poll. And Miami drivers are the worst in America.

LALLY: [*to the audience*] Three serious bicycle accidents.

ALEX: Yeah, a lot a' the time, they deliberately try to hit us. You know, it's the cars against the bikes, but I go both ways.

LALLY: [*to the audience*] Down the highway through Virginia, the neighbourhoods and shopping malls in the hazy distance.

His father and his grandfather had both spent most of their adult lives in jail.

ALEX: Well, you know Miami in the eighties, you ever watched a movie called *Cocaine Cowboys*? It's a great movie. Documentary. It's just the way it was, so easy to make money, for everybody, you know, and the whole system was corrupt so no-one really cared. It was too easy not to do it.

LALLY: [*to the audience*] We drive through the hills of North Carolina. Through the tree-filled city of Charlotte. Alex's cousin had recently been shot thirteen times to death by police.

ALEX: It's a joke. He didn't do anything. They just wanted to kill him. And there's nothing anyone can do about it.

LALLY: So they just walked up to him and shot him?

ALEX: They say he was armed, but he wasn't. And they killed him. That's why I moved to New York. Too sad.

LALLY: [*to the audience*] We speed through South Carolina and into Georgia. And he, himself, had recently been beaten up by the police.

ALEX: I got this big dog, a pit bull, and I was walking it and this police car is blocking the path where I gotta walk it, so I have to lift up this heavy, heavy dog, up over their roadblock that they put up, and

ACT THREE 61

they're all just looking. So I say, 'You want to help me lift my dog, you're not doing nothing and it's because of you I have to lift it'. They mouth off at me and I mouth off back and next thing you know, they're beating up on me. My mom said I'm lucky to be alive, but I knew I'd be okay because I got lighter skin than my cousin. Hey, so you've really never learned how to drive?

LALLY: No. It just never seemed like any of my business.

ALEX: You want to have a go now?

LALLY: No. I don't have my learners, so it would be breaking the law. I'm terrified of breaking the law.

ALEX: You're a white girl, no-one'll pull you over.

LALLY: It's more the crashing I'm worried about.

ALEX: Well, the offer's on the table. I taught my mother how to drive at forty-seven.

LALLY: Thank you. Maybe in the next life.

[*To the audience*] And then suddenly, I can see, the difference in the plants. Feel the soft, humid air holding me. We stop talking. And I breathe it in. The dark dawn is pressed up against the car windows. Wind whips the glass. Keep driving. Keep driving.

She looks out the window.

[*To the audience*] I know it. Before I even see the road signs. This is Miami. We pass the beach. And then I start to recognise the streets. A hill we used to roll down next to a bridge. The things you remember. And then we go and deeper and deeper. Towards Kendall. The suburban strip malls. The Publix shopping centre. That's where my mum got me my Archie comics. And then my neighbourhood—the cul-de-sacs. I know these cul-de-sacs. I'm so happy I feel like I'll cry.

[*To* ALEX] Wow. This is familiar. It remembered it like a tropical Smurf Village. And that's what it actually is.

ALEX: So this your street?

LALLY: No, this isn't it.

[*To the audience*] And then we drive into the next one. The houses are exactly the same as I remembered, except maybe more Latin-looking. There are so many new trees, and some that I remembered are gone. Neighbours who I had completely forgotten rush back into my mind at seeing their houses.

[*To* ALEX] I can't believe it. This is it. This is my street! That's where my friend Jessica lived—that's the house where I watched *The Neverending Story* for the first time, that's the house where the drug dealer with the gold convertible lived. And that's my house.

[*To the audience*] Alex parks outside of my house. A man in his fifties is boarding up the windows of the house. I guess for when the hurricane comes.

ALEX: [*nodding in the direction of the guy*] Cuban.

LALLY: I'm gonna ask him if I can go into the house.

ALEX: Maybe I should do the talking.

LALLY: That's so nice of you, but I feel like that's asking too much. After all, it is my house.

ALEX: You can try.

    LALLY *approaches the* CUBAN MAN.

LALLY: Hello, sir. My name is Lally and I used to live in this house.

He looks back at her blankly. And indicates that he doesn't speak English.

CUBAN MAN: No English.

LALLY: Oh. Have no *Española*. Sorry. I'm so embarrassed about it. I'm going to take lessons.

    She turns to ALEX.

Maybe you better talk to him after all.

    ALEX *speaks in rapid Spanish to him. He turns to* LALLY.

ALEX: He wants to know what you want in the house.

LALLY: Tell him I used to live here. Twenty-seven years ago. I'm thirty-five now.

    ALEX *speaks in Spanish to the man. He turns back to* LALLY.

ALEX: He said he doesn't believe you. He says there's no way you're thirty-five.

LALLY: Tell him I said *mucho gracias*. But it's true. And I just—I need to see inside the house—before it's too late. And it won't take me long. I'll just go in and out. I just need to go inside my house.

    ALEX *and the* CUBAN MAN *speak in Spanish.*

ALEX: He wants to know what it is you're looking for.

ACT THREE

LALLY: I don't know. I just want to see my house.

> ALEX *tells the* CUBAN MAN. *He shakes his head and says something.*

ALEX: No disrespect, but he said he thinks you're on drugs. Or maybe have a mental illness.

LALLY: I know it seems crazy. But if I could just go into my house just once. Please.

> *The* CUBAN MAN *shakes his head. He begins to go back to boarding up the windows.*

> LALLY *looks at him, and then runs towards the front door. The* CUBAN MAN *jumps in front of her. He starts yelling out for the police in Spanish.*

ALEX: We better go.

LALLY: Let me in my house! You have to let me in my house! Please let me in my house.

ALEX: He's calling the neighbourhood security guard. They carry guns. We better go.

LALLY: No. I can't go. You go. Thank you. But I'm not going.

> *A* SECURITY GUARD *comes.*

SECURITY GUARD: What's going on here?

LALLY: I need to go into my house.

SECURITY GUARD [*to* ALEX] Are you two together?

ALEX: I'm just her Uber driver. I think she might be having some sort of episode.

SECURITY GUARD: Ma'am, you have to leave now.

LALLY: Not until you let me into my house.

SECURITY GUARD: Are you nuts? This is not your house. This house belongs to Alejándro and his family. Have you got anywhere else to go? What about home?

LALLY: I thought this was home.

SECURITY GUARD: Well, I don't think it is. Anymore.

LALLY: [*to the audience*] Lightning bolts, thunder shouts across the sky. It begins to pour down rain.

No. I didn't come this far to not go home.

She stands up and runs inside the house. The SECURITY GUARD *chases her. Lightning cracks.*

END OF ACT THREE

ACT FOUR

SCENE ONE

The hurricane opens up over Miami. A dark black cloud. The whiteness of the city turns storm grey. The low rumbling and then crackling of thunder.

LALLY: [*to the audience*] I run into my old house. Besides the Cuban man's family watching the news, the TV room is exactly the same.

She runs past them, trying to hide.

The CUBAN MAN *comes racing in, yells to his family:*

CUBAN MAN: [*in Spanish*] Did you see her?!

MOTHER-IN-LAW: [*in Spanish*] Shut up, we're watching the television!

LALLY *sprints out from behind the couch and towards the back of the house. The* CUBAN MAN *shakes his head and chases after her.*

Thunder cracks. Rain begins to slide down the windows.

LALLY: [*to the audience, as she runs*] They've changed the carpet and the tiles. But the rooms—the rooms are exactly the same shape. Living room—check. Kitchen—check. Hallway—check. Me and my brother's bedroom—check. I make it into the master bedroom. Where my parents used to sleep. It's the same. I run into the ensuite to hide.

SECURITY GUARD: Come out with your hands up.

He holds his gun out. Lightning cracks.

LALLY: [*to the audience*] I slam the ensuite door shut and lock it.

SECURITY GUARD: Open up! Or we'll shoot!

They bang on the door. LALLY *lies on the floor and closes her eyes. A voice begins to count.*

PANTHER: One. Two. Three. Four. Five. Six. Seven. Eight. Nine. Ten.

LALLY: [*to the audience*] And a different door opens. To reveal a secret room behind the ensuite. And there—there is the—

PANTHER: Panther. And there is the panther.

LALLY: You're here.

PANTHER: I've been here for twenty-eight years. Ever since you left. Waiting for you. I've kept such a low profile. I used to creep out sometimes just before dawn. But people would sight me. There were rumours for a while that a panther made it into town from the Everglades. But it's been so long now, that no-one, not even the sighters really believe that I'm real anymore. I hardly believed it myself. Why didn't you come back sooner?

LALLY: I thought you were best friends with Corey.

PANTHER: Didn't you see me crying on the other side of the school? Because you were leaving? And then I came back here and you were already gone.

LALLY: Why didn't you tell me? Why didn't you tell me you were sad too?

PANTHER: Why didn't you know? If we were really soulmates—then you should have known.

LALLY: Well, now I'm back. And now I know.

PANTHER: Why didn't you come back before? What were you doing, Lally? What were you doing all that time that you were away from me? What was so important that it kept you from me?

LALLY: We moved to Australia. I went to school. I became a writer. I fell in love.

PANTHER: I needed you.

LALLY: I need you too. I'm in trouble. Can't you see I'm in trouble? I feel like I'm losing my mind. And I need you—you're the only one who can help me.

PANTHER: I'm so hungry.

LALLY: We'll find you food.

PANTHER: It's too late. Because the world is ending. You came back too late.

LALLY: It's not too late. We're both here. We're both alive. There's still hope.

PANTHER: Hope? You really are losing your mind. There's no hope left. All that's left is my hunger. I'm sorry, but I'm going to have to eat you.

LALLY: No! I came so far. To be with you.

PANTHER: And you will be.

The PANTHER *moves towards her.*

ACT FOUR 67

LALLY: Fine. Eat me. But first, let's play hide and seek.
PANTHER: There's nowhere left to hide in Miami. It's all been developed. Where is the long grass? Where are the alligator reeds? Nowhere. There's nowhere to hide. Except for this secret room. And I'm already here. So I'll eat you now.
LALLY: Please, can we be best friends instead?
PANTHER: Tempting. But no. The storm has started. The water is coming. Don't you know by now? Our love is cursed.

Thunder.

LALLY: No! Because look.

She points towards the audience.

BELLA *and her* ASSISTANT *are walking up the mountain. The* ASSISTANT *is carrying a huge bag of crystals and candles. The sky is dark purple. With lightning cracks across it. The trees bend in the wind. Snow begins to fall past the lightning, and in its flashes it turns on like thousands of flakes of chandeliers.* BELLA, *being obese and chronically unfit, has to stop every few moments and wheeze. Her* ASSISTANT, *though almost doubled over with the weight of the crystals and candles, never falters and offers* BELLA *his hand.*

BELLA: I'm okay. I got it, I got it.

She swats his hand away, takes a deep wheeze and then continues up the mountain. She speaks in between wheezes.

I told her this is a big job. Really we should only do this for two thousand minimum. Fifteen hundred—what was I nuts? That means I gotta give you a reduced fee. I don't even get no fee. It barely covers expenses. I shouldn'ta agreed. But she's a regular customer. And in these financial times …
ASSISTANT: Doing business is good for business.
BELLA: Yeah, but I'm too old for this. Oh shoot, looks like the blizzard is settin' in too. We'll be lucky if we get out of this alive ourselves.
ASSISTANT: We've almost reached the top.
BELLA: You been sayin' that for two hours now. I knew we shoulda brought the mule.
ASSISTANT: Well, I hope this client will be happy. That's all I can say.

BELLA: Eh. They never are. It's always a sob story with every client, sayin' I'm overchargin' them. Well, don't ask for something if you ain't prepared to pay the price.
ASSISTANT: I never felt a storm coming this heavy. We shouldn't be walking up here, should we, boss?
BELLA: It's our fate. Gotta listen to our fate.
ASSISTANT: Well, you're the master. Woulda been good if our fate hadn't short-changed us though. At least the full two thousand, you know?
BELLA: Tell me about it.
ASSISTANT: I learnt more from you than anyone I know. You know that?
BELLA: I ain't dead. I just got a weight problem and this mountain is kicking my ass. Keeps me warm though. Come on. Keep walkin'. Let's get rid of her curse.

They keep walking up the mountain. LALLY *speaks to the* PANTHER.

LALLY: You see. We're cured. It's a new beginning.
PANTHER: But look, we're out of time. The taxi driver is arriving in Miami.

The NEW YORK TAXI DRIVER *and her family get out of their car at a hotel in Miami. There's a lot of them. Some of them carry small bags. One of them pushes her husband in a wheelchair. She goes up to reception.*

RECEPTIONIST: Do you have a booking?
NEW YORK TAXI DRIVER: We sure do. Had one for the past year. Under Edgars.

He looks in his computer.

RECEPTIONIST: Okay. This is quite a long booking you've got here.
NEW YORK TAXI DRIVER: Yes. We planned ahead.
RECEPTIONIST: And how will you be paying?
NEW YORK TAXI DRIVER: In cash.

She takes out wads of cash.

RECEPTIONIST: Wow.
NEW YORK TAXI DRIVER: Tips from the past eleven years.
RECEPTIONIST: You know there's a hurricane coming in. We're going to keep our guests alerted on safety. But we don't recommend going to the beach. Sorry you're arrived for such terrible weather.

NEW YORK TAXI DRIVER: Don't be sorry. It couldn't be more perfect.

Back to LALLY *and the* PANTHER.

PANTHER: You see, it's too late. Ten, nine, eight, seven, six, five, four, three, two, one. I found you.
LALLY: Please. Don't eat me. Please marry me instead. And we'll go and find Atlantis.
PANTHER: You want to find Atlantis?
LALLY: Yes.
PANTHER: I'll take you there.
LALLY: And you'll marry me.
PANTHER: Yes.

Banging on the door. The door opens. The SECURITY GUARD *is there with a gun.*

SECURITY GUARD: What the fuck?

He shoots. He gets the PANTHER *in the side.* LALLY *screams. The* PANTHER *slashes the* SECURITY GUARD*'s throat with his claw. The* PANTHER *falls back.* LALLY *runs over to it.*

LALLY: Are you okay?
PANTHER: It's just a flesh wound. Come on.

The PANTHER *stands up.*

CUBAN MAN: [*in Spanish*] Jesus, save me.
PANTHER: I don't speak Spanish. But I understand it. Can you understand me?
CUBAN MAN: [*in Spanish*] A little.
PANTHER: I want to take your boat.
CUBAN MAN: [*in Spanish*] I'll make you a deal.
PANTHER: Yes?
CUBAN MAN: [*in Spanish*] You want the boat, then eat my mother-in-law. And go.
PANTHER: You haven't known me all these years. But I have considered you a friend.

The PANTHER *nods. He makes his way through the ensuite, through the bedroom, down the hall.*

CUBAN MAN: [*in Spanish*] Good luck.
LALLY: Thank you.

The sound of the PANTHER *growling in the living room. The sound of a woman screaming. Of several people screaming. The sound of the* CUBAN MAN'S WIFE *screaming out:*

CUBAN MAN'S WIFE: [*offstage, in Spanish*] No no no no! It's got Mama! That panther has got Mama!

Rain down the windows. The water is rising. Thunder. Lightning. Wind. The PANTHER *comes back in, he grabs* LALLY's *hand.*

PANTHER: Come.

They race through the rain to the motor boat in the backyard.

SCENE TWO

LALLY: [*to the audience*] The rain fills up my old backyard fast. My cul-de-sac is gone in a heartbeat. But I don't care. Because I got what I came for. We set off in the motor boat.

LALLY and the PANTHER sit next to each other in the motor boat, holding hands.

PANTHER: I'd almost given up on you. On having children. On finding love. I thought I was always going to be alone. And then, suddenly. In the moment before it was too late, there you are.

LALLY: So we're really going to mate? We're really going to have children?

PANTHER: Yes.

LALLY: [*to the audience*] The water rises quickly. And we sail. Over the roofs of townhouses. Over car dealerships with the glint of hoods and windows of new cars rippling through the water. Over the shopping malls and drawbridges, over supermarkets and parking lots. The panther is bleeding in the boat.

LALLY: Are you okay?

PANTHER: Yes. A little blood is healthy.

LALLY: [*to the audience*] And then we see Bella's daughter and Electra, both floating on some driftwood. They are being circled by sharks and alligators.

ELECTRA: This must be the Gulf of Mexico. We've floated so far.

BELLA'S DAUGHTER: Oh, my God—what's that down there?

ELECTRA looks down through the water.

ACT FOUR

ELECTRA: Now I don't fucking believe it.
BELLA'S DAUGHTER: Oh, my God. I know what it is. It's Atlantis. That land under the sea. We've discovered it.
ELECTRA: Nah, this ain't Atlantis. It's Miami. It's beautiful. Look at the hotels. How they glisten.
BELLA'S DAUGHTER: It's like crystals. My mom would have loved this.

LALLY calls out to them.

LALLY: Hey, you guys.
ELECTRA: Oh, hey. Thanks for the good Airbnb review. I'm glad I saw you again. I wanted to tell you, I'm not sad anymore. I'm so happy being with myself. And I wanted to thank you for taking care of my dog. Unfortunately, a barracuda ate her. But I wish I'd known that back then. That I was enough. I would have just lived my life. Without feeling so lonely—so left behind.
BELLA'S DAUGHTER: The painful and futile grip of desire.
ELECTRA: What do you mean by that?
BELLA'S DAUGHTER: Just something that used to come into my head when I'd hear my mom talking to her clients.

LALLY's mobile phone rings. LALLY and the PANTHER continue to float away.

LALLY: Dave … Sorry guys, I just have to take this. Hello? Dave? [*Listens*] I've been okay. How about you? Are you okay? I've thought about you a lot. I wanted to say, I'm sorry that I blamed you for it not working out with us. It wasn't your fault. You weren't available. But I wasn't either. Take care.

She nestles into the PANTHER.
A cruise ship passes. Electra looks up at it. Through one of the little circle windows, Kanye West looks out. He calls out to her.
KANYE: Dammit—I've been looking for you for a long time.
ELECTRA: What about Kim?
KANYE: Don't tell me you haven't been passing the time in your own way.
ELECTRA: Yeah. But now it's our time. Finally.

ELECTRA and BELLA'S DAUGHTER board the ship. LALLY and the PANTHER sail on.

SCENE THREE

LALLY: [*to the audience*] We pass Diego on a yacht.
DIEGO: Hey, you guys okay?
LALLY: Nice yacht.
DIEGO: Yeah, I got it for high sales in Kyani. Dude, you're not looking so good. Have a miracle health drink.

>DIEGO *throws them a Kyani.*

PANTHER: Thank you.

>*He takes a sip.*

Wow. This really lifts my energy.
DIEGO: Yeah, I got herpes after having sex with her.

>*He points to* LALLY.

But Kyani cured it.
LALLY: But you gave me herpes!
DIEGO: No. I never had it. A week after seeing you, I got all these little cuts on my dick. You can carry it in your system for years without knowing. But I forgive you. Because Kyani cured me.
PANTHER: But isn't herpes incurable?
DIEGO: It's a miracle. So, you want to join?
PANTHER: Maybe later. Thank you.
DIEGO: All you gotta do is get three friends to join.
PANTHER: Lally's my only friend.
DIEGO: Oh, well. Maybe later.
LALLY: [*to the audience*] And we drift apart. In the Stonebridge Retirement Village, Pop-Op sits alone. The rain dripping down the walls. The wind blowing into the room.
POP-OP: Dossie, are you here? I'm coming, baby.

>*He sings 'September Song'.*

SCENE FOUR

As POP-OP *sings 'September Song',* LALLY *and the* PANTHER *sail across America, holding hands.*

The PANTHER *is getting weaker and weaker.*

ACT FOUR

LALLY: Are you worried about what he said?
PANTHER: Herpes? No. Herpes can't kill me.
LALLY: [*to the audience*] That's when you know you're with your soulmate.
PANTHER: Are you worried that my dick has barbs?
LALLY: A little.
PANTHER: I'll be as gentle as I can. But you have to understand, all love has some pain. Afterwards, if I fall asleep and we haven't hit land, wake me up. I don't want to miss any of this. Now, mate with me.
LALLY: Okay.

[*To the audience*] The panther and I mate on the boat as we sail across Florida, Alabama, Mississippi, New Orleans, Texas, New Mexico. He whispers in my ear and I think he's about to talk dirty, but instead he tells me about every single day that we were apart. What time he woke up in the morning. What chores he did. What books he read. What he thought. What he ate. And what he imagined I was doing. I leave my body and go into his. He leaves his and comes into mine. We go back and forth between ourselves with the rocking of the boat.

The water starts to shallow as we get into Arizona. We can see the tops of houses and cars beneath, tree branches billowing in the current like it's the breeze. The panther falls asleep beside me. I don't wake him up, even though I told him I would. He looks so tired. When we reach Nevada, the water trickles out and it's gone. It's just desert. Our boat stops suddenly, beached in the sand.

The PANTHER *jolts awake. He goes to sit up, but he's weak.*

PANTHER: We're here. Las Vegas. Look at the lights.
LALLY: Wow. Did you bring me to Vegas to marry me?
PANTHER: I wanted to.
LALLY: I've always dreamed of getting married in Vegas.
PANTHER: I know. But I think you'll have to make the rest of the trip alone.
LALLY: [*to the audience*] I look down and the bottom of the boat is filled with the panther's blood. I hadn't noticed how much he was bleeding as we mated.

[*To the* PANTHER] No. I'll carry you.
PANTHER: Lally, I'm dying.

LALLY: No. I can't live without you. I don't want to be alone again.
PANTHER: You won't. You're pregnant. With me. You always will be.
LALLY: Will I have a baby?
PANTHER: Our story will live inside you. My words tucked into your womb, feeding off of your life. There are different ways to be a mother.
LALLY: But I wanted something real.
PANTHER: A story is real. Hope is real. I see that now. I have something for you here in Vegas. I wanted to take you after we were married. But now you'll have to go on.
LALLY: What is it?
PANTHER: What you've been looking for. Atlantis.
LALLY: Atlantis is here?
PANTHER: Yes. Go and find it. Take my coat. It's the desert. But the nights get cold.

> *The* PANTHER *hands* LALLY *a purple, faux fur shaggy, cheap-looking, short coat. She puts it on, holds herself tight in it.*

LALLY: [*to the audience*] The water begins to lap up on the boat. The panther looks in my eyes as the waves pull him back out again, towards Miami. I know his eyes are empty now. But I hold their gaze until I can't see the boat anymore. And then I walk across the desert, in search of Atlantis.

It doesn't take me long.

Caesar's Palace Casino pulsates past me, first the opulent card tables, the Roman-themed pokie machines and then the shining shop windows, the blue always just pre-evening fake sky above, the white clouds resemble the clouds in 'The Simpsons', the floor that looks like money welcoming our feet. I walk, wrapped up in the panther's coat. It's me and the panther. I don't know where we're walking, but the casino leads us. I'm tired in that way you get after being in a shopping mall too long and that same kind of thirsty too.

But then, as I reach the end of the casino mall, there it is. Atlantis. A huge fountain at the end of the shopping area inside the casino. It has Atlantis written on it. Behind the fountain is an aquarium that circles around and children run following the stingrays and finding Nemo-type fish as they swim round.

ACT FOUR

High up on the walls, above the cheesecake factory and souvenir store, are projections of schools of fish, then sunken ships, lost treasure, anything you could picture under the sea.

> LALLY *stands eating an ice-cream in her purple fake fur coat.*
>
> ANNOUNCEMENT: *'Ladies and gentlemen, the Caesar's Palace four p.m. 'Fall of Atlantis' show will now begin. Please stand back from the stage to avoid getting wet or being burnt by the flames. You can film, but please, keep your phones low so as not to obstruct the view of other audience members.'*
>
> *A statue rises from the fountain. A king, with a dragon. And then two more. His son and daughter. Water and fire.*
>
> STATUE: *'I am Atlas, King of Atlantis. And I must see which of my children shall become ruler.'*
>
> *A* COWGIRL *in the audience smiles at* LALLY.

COWGIRL: You seen this show before?
LALLY: No. It's my first time.
COWGIRL: I seen it about six times. My son drags me here every hour. He loves it.
LALLY: That's funny.
COWGIRL: You here with your kids?
LALLY: No. I'm … a writer.
COWGIRL: Well, that's okay— Same purpose, right? Share something of yourself with the world. Try and take care of it and make it so that other people like it.
LALLY: Yeah. I hope so.
COWGIRL: I used to feel that way about my horses. Where did you come from?
LALLY: Miami.
COWGIRL: Long flight.
LALLY: I drove.
COWGIRL: You didn't! Not from Miami.
LALLY: I just got my licence there. I paid for lessons with an Uber driver. And as soon as I passed my test, I rented a car and drove here. My first time driving on my own.
COWGIRL: Well, good for you. I got a DUI last year. Suspended my goddamn license. I asked them how I was supposed to drive my son to

school and they said I shoulda thought a that before I drove him to the waterslide park drunk—but dammit, he wanted to go. Can't they see I'm a good mother?

Something happens on the Atlantis stage.

Whoa! Every time that splash gets me! Surprises me every damn time! No matter how much I see this show, that splash. What are you writing about now?

LALLY: Funnily enough, this.

COWGIRL: Will I be in it?

LALLY: Yes.

COWGIRL: I'm famous! Well, I better find my son. He keeps wandering off to that aquarium. Vegas, huh. I love this place. I like that fake Venice better than the real Venice. And fake Paris better than the real Paris. And this fake Atlantis—I'll bet it's better than the real Atlantis.

LALLY: Maybe they're all real.

COWGIRL: Well, it's just as hard to find as the real one. You get lost as hell in Caesar's Palace.

LALLY: Yeah.

COWGIRL: But we found it. We both got to Atlantis.

LALLY: Yeah.

COWGIRL: Well, I better find my son before he kills a stingray. Enjoy the show.

LALLY: You too.

[*To the audience*] King Atlas's children fight back and forth about who should be the ruler. His daughter uses water and it sprays from the stage. His son uses fire and for those close to the stage, it's very hot. They fight until the gods tire of them and the whole of Atlantis is swallowed up by the sea. A dragon opens its wings behind King Atlas. And then they're all gone. Atlantis is lost. But the show happens every hour on the hour. So it will be found again.

THE END

Belvoir presents

ATLANTIS

By **LALLY KATZ**
Director **ROSEMARY MYERS**

This production of Atlantis *opened at Belvoir St Theatre on Wednesday 1 November 2017.*

Set & Costume Designer **JONATHON OXLADE**
Lighting Designer **DAMIEN COOPER**
Composer & Sound Designer **HARRY COVILL**
Dialect Coach **PAIGE WALKER**
Movement Director **SARA BLACK**
Production Manager **SALLY WITHNELL**
Technical Manager **AIDEN BRENNAN**
Deputy Production Manager **ROXZAN BOWES**
Stage Manager **KEIREN SMITH**
Assistant Stage Manager **GEORGIANE DEAL**
Senior Technician **RAINE PAUL**

With
PAULA ARUNDELL
LUCIA MASTRANTONE
AMBER McMAHON
HAZEM SHAMMAS
MATTHEW WHITTET

Atlantis is supported by
The Hive and The Honey Bs.

Lucia Mastrantone

We acknowledge the Gadigal people of the Eora nation who are the traditional custodians of the land on which Belvoir St Theatre is built. We also pay respect to the elders past and present.

PRODUCTION THANKS
Chloe Greaves, Ren Kenward, Brooke Kiss, Matthew McLaughlin, Michael McStay

PHOTOGRAPHY
Brett Boardman

DESIGN
Alphabet Studio

Lally Katz

WRITER'S NOTE

Lally Katz

Thanks so much for coming to see *Atlantis*. I really hope you enjoy it. I've really enjoyed writing it and I love working at Belvoir. I'm so grateful that they've made this play happen.

The idea for *Atlantis* came from a conversation I had with an oceanographer in my grandparents' retirement home in 2012 about rising sea levels, and something a taxi driver told me in 2011 about her belief in Atlantis. But you'll see that in the play.

This is a story made up of a lot of different characters and stories that were part of my life over the past five or so years. All of them changed me in some way and then became part of my life story. I hope you will love them like I have loved them.

The character of 'Lally' says in the beginning of the play that everything in it is based on truth and all the characters in it are based on real people. This is true and not true, because it is still a story. In the play, time and places have morphed. Two people from life have sometimes become one character in the play. Events are changed and rearranged to fit together into scenes. Dialogue has been invented and rewritten. Some of it is exactly true, as I remember it. But of course, memory is a tricky thing and can't always be trusted as true.

Certain weather events that I wrote about in the play actually began to occur during our rehearsal period. Any similarity is purely coincidence: Except that it is what climate scientists (including the oceanographer) have been predicting.

I've had many collaborators since beginning work on this in 2012. I'd like to thank all the actors who participated in the workshops and gave so much. Many great minds have provided invaluable dramaturgy to the script, but I'd like to particularly thank: Eamon Flack, Rosemary Myers, Chris Drummond, Anthea Williams, Ben Chessell and Luke Mullins.

I've loved working with the brilliant director Rose Myers and the incredible cast and crew on this adventure.

I'd like to thank Anita Jacoby for believing in this project and supporting it from the beginning and coming to the workshops. And I'd like to thank my friends and Belvoir supporters The Hive and The Honey Bs for their support. It means a lot.

Thank you to my agents and thanks to Christian Nardi for forgiving me for leaving town for two months to rehearse this play.

And finally, thank you to my family for always being good sports about ending up in my work. And to my brother Michael, for his lifelong, unwavering friendship and support.

DIRECTOR'S NOTE

Rosemary Myers

I think Lally Katz is totally brilliant so I was excited and deeply honoured when Eamon Flack asked me to consider directing her new work, *Atlantis*, for the 2017 Belvoir season. I read the draft on a flight to America, which proved particularly appropriate, and I laughed out loud at its continual surprises, inspired by Lally's unique theatrical voice. The play is a road trip for our time and it explores ideas with potent metaphors and astounding characters.

I don't want to give too much away before you experience it for yourself, but this work is a testament to the way Lally's life and art are deeply intertwined. We meet a woman grappling with her own ticking clock living in a world on a countdown. It is about an eternal optimist reconciling dreams with reality, and it is a Lally Katz message of hope.

The flair Lally exhibits rendering her imaginings on the page pose exciting challenges for the team tasked with delivering them to the stage. I have been happy to be accompanied in this endeavour by the boundless talent of some of my absolute favourite collaborators: the incredible Amber, Jonathon, Matthew and Harry. This is my second time working with the wonderful Hazem and the first with the creative dexterity of Lucia, the rigour of Paula and the absolute expertise of Damien. Thank you also to Eamon for his insightful dramaturgy, our stage manager Keiren and ASM Georgie for their care, coordination and cakes, to Paige and Sara for their invaluable contribution and to all of the wonderful Belvoir team across production, marketing and admin.

Thank you also to Kaye Weeks and the team at Windmill Theatre Co for their support, which made it possible for me to be part of this production.

Our rehearsal room has been full of laughter and revelation as we realise the premiere production of this original play - it is the work that drives us as makers of theatre.

I hope you enjoy the ride as much as I have.

Rose

Rosemary Myers

BIOGRAPHIES

LALLY KATZ Writer

Lally is one of the most-produced playwrights in Australia. For Belvoir, Lally has written *The Dog / The Cat*, *Back at the Dojo*, *Stories I Want to Tell You in Person* in which she also starred, and *Neighbourhood Watch*. Lally has performed *Stories I Want to Tell You in Person* in New York, India, Mexico, Brisbane, Adelaide and Albury, and it was also adapted for screen by ABC, with Lally reprising her starring role. She is currently adapting her play *Neighbourhood Watch* as a feature film with Gillian Armstrong attached to direct. Her plays *The Black Swan of Trespass* and *The Eisteddfod* (Stuck Pigs Squealing) were part of Belvoir's B Sharp seasons in 2005 and 2007, and both toured to New York. In 2015, Lally wrote the libretto for the opera adaptation of John Marsden's *The Rabbits*, which was a sell-out hit at the Perth International Arts Festival, Melbourne International Arts Festival and Sydney Festival. Lally's other writing credits include *The Eisteddfod* (Black Swan State Theatre Company); *Timeshare*, *Goodbye Vaudeville Charlie Mudd*, *A Golem Story*, *Criminology* (Malthouse Theatre); *The Mysteries: Genesis*, *Frankenstein*, *Waikiki Palace*, *Hip Hip Hooray* (Sydney Theatre Company); *Minnie and Liraz*, *Apocalypse Bear Trilogy* and *Return to Earth* (Melbourne Theatre Company). For TV, Lally has written episodes of *Wentworth*, *The Elephant Princess* and *Spirited*. She has won two Victorian Premier's Literary Awards, a New York International Fringe Festival Award and several Green Room Awards. Lally has been awarded a Churchill Fellowship, a British Council Realise Your Dreams grant and a playwriting grant from The Australian Writers' Foundation.

ROSEMARY MYERS Director

Rose is currently the Artistic Director of Windmill Theatre Co. A multi-Helpmann award winner, her productions regularly visit leading stages and festivals around Australia and the world. Her directing credits for Windmill include *Pinocchio* and *Rumpelstiltskin* (co-productions with State Theatre Company South Australia), *The Wizard of Oz*, *Fugitive*, *School Dance*, *Big Bad Wolf* and *Girl Asleep*. Prior to Windmill, Rosemary was the Artistic Director of Arena Theatre Company where she directed works including *Criminology*, *Play Dirty*, *Eat Your Young*, *Panacea*, *Autopsy* and *Schnorky the Wave Puncher*. She was also the 2010 Artistic Director of Queensland Performing Arts Centre's Out of the Box Festival, the Artistic Director of the Melbourne University Union Theatre and a Creative Director for the 2006 Melbourne Commonwealth Games Ceremony. In 2015, she directed her first feature film *Girl Asleep* which received seven AACTA nominations, was selected to open the Berlinale Generation 14plus, and won multiple awards including The Age Critics Award at MIFF, the Cinefest Oz Film Prize, the Seattle Film Festival Grand Jury Prize and the Adelaide Film Festival Foxtel Audience Award. In 2017 Rosemary was awarded the Australia Council Theatre Award.

Hazem Shammas

Lucia Mastrantone
& Amber McMahon

PAULA ARUNDELL Electra & Others

For Belvoir, **Paula** has appeared in *Mr Burns*, *Mother Courage and Her Children*, *Angels in America Parts One* and *Two*, *Peter Pan*, *Death of a Salesman*, *Gethsemane*, *Scorched*, *Snugglepot and Cuddlepie*, *Paul*, *Peribanez* and *The Threepenny Opera*. Other theatre credits include *A Midsummer Night's Dream*, *Disgraced*, *Suddenly Last Summer*, *Macbeth*, *Under Milk Wood*, *The Mirage*, *Honour*, *Blackbird*, *Love Lies Bleeding*, *Life is a Dream*, *The Three Sisters*, *The White Devil*, *Attempts on Her Life*, *Love for Love*, *Julius Caesar* (Sydney Theatre Company); *The Real and Imagined History of The Elephant Man* (Malthouse Theatre); *Clybourne Park*, *Interactive World Theatre*, *Are You There?* (Ensemble); *The Bleeding Tree*, *Clark in Sarajevo* (Griffin); *Oedipus Rex*, *Symphony of Psalms* (Sydney Festival); *Three Furies* (Sydney Festival/Auckland Festival); *Spiders from Mars* (Australian Museum); *Elegies for Punks, Angels and Raging Queens* (Mardi Gras); *The Torrens*, *Night Letters* (State Theatre Company South Australia); *The Servant of Two Masters*, *Hippolytus*, *Antony and Cleopatra*, *Henry V*, *The Tempest*, *Much Ado About Nothing* (Bell Shakespeare); *Company* and *Measure For Measure* (Melbourne Theatre Company). Paula's film credits include *Harmony*, *Gods of Egypt*, *Disgrace*, *Bad Eggs*, *Sample People* and *Diana & Me* and she performed the title song vocal for *Candy*. Her TV credits include *Top of the Lake: China Girl*, *Hunters*, *The Time of Our Lives*, *Slide*, *Farscape*, *All Saints*, *Murder Call*, *Water Rats*, *The Alice* and *Love My Way*. Paula has won numerous awards including a 2016 Helpmann Award for Best Female Actor for her performance in *The Bleeding Tree*. Paula can be seen in the upcoming shows *Sami in Paradise* and *An Enemy of the People* at Belvoir.

SARA BLACK Movement Director

With a Bachelor of Dance from VCA, **Sara** has worked as a choreographer, performer, teacher and collaborator in Australia and internationally over the past 12 years. Her choreographic credits include *Jasper Jones*, *Seventeen*, *Peter Pan* (Belvoir); *Girls Like That* (ATYP); *#KillAllMen* (NIDA); *The Incredible Here and Now* (NToP); *Seven Deadly Sins* (Out of the Shadows Festival); *Taction* (Sydney Dance Company PPY); *Act of Contact* (QL2); *E-volve* (CDDC); *Pitch Black* (Seekae live event); *Sensation*, *Trigger*, *Action* (Flipside); and *Fresh Produce* (Rogue, Next Wave Festival Event). Her assistant choreographic credits include *Obsidian* (Iceland Dance Company); Eddie Perfect's *Shane Warne the Musical*; and *Woyzeck* (Malthouse Theatre). Sara's short works include *Value for Money* (London premiere); *Untitled* (ReadyMade Happy hour); *InAnimate* (Lucy Guerin Inc); and *Parental Guidance Recommended* (Dancehouse). As a founding member of Rogue dance collective, Sara co-created and choreographed new works *Puck*, *Ocular Proof* and *Persona*. Over the last 11 years she has performed and collaborated with Punchdrunk (UK), Protein Dance (UK), The Australian Ballet, Lucy Guerin Inc, NYID (David Pledger) and as a main collaborator and performer for Gideon Obarzanek's Chunky Move where she toured extensively internationally. In 2008 she received a Helpmann Award for Best Performer in a Dance or Physical Theatre Work and has since been nominated for two Green Room Awards in the same category. Sara has worked extensively with both Australian and international independent artists including Narelle Benjamin, Erna Omarsdottir, Damien Jalet, Martin Del Amo, Elissa Goodrich, Bagryana Popov, Stephanie Lake, Lloyd Newson, Wendy Houstoun, Carlee Mellow, Antony Hamilton and Byron Perry.

DAMIEN COOPER Lighting Designer

Damien works internationally across theatre, opera and dance. His work for Belvoir includes *Mark Colvin's Kidney*, *The Dog / The Cat*, *The Great Fire*, *Radiance*, *The Glass Menagerie*, *Coranderrk*, *Miss Julie*, *Stories I Want to Tell You in Person*, *Cat on a Hot Tin Roof*, *Peter Pan*, *Private Lives*, *Conversation Piece*, *Strange Interlude*, *Summer of the Seventeenth Doll*, *Neighbourhood Watch*, *The Seagull*, *Gethsemane*, *Keating!*, *Toy Symphony*, *Peribanez*, *Stuff Happens*, *The Chairs*, *The Spook*, *In Our Name*, *The Underpants*, *The Ham Funeral* and *Exit the King* (including the Broadway production with Geoffrey Rush and Susan Sarandon). His other theatre credits include *Dinner*, *Disgraced*, *Orlando*, *Arcadia*, *A Midsummer Night's Dream*, *The Golden Age*, *Suddenly Last Summer*, *The Women of Troy*, *The Lost Echo*, *Riflemind*, *Tot Mom* (Sydney Theatre Company); *Macbeth* and *The Tempest* (Bell Shakespeare). For opera, Damien's designs include *Der Ring des Nibelungen*, *Aida*, *Cosi Fan Tutte*, *The Merry Widow* (Opera Australia); *Peter Grimes* (Opera Australia/Canadian Opera Company/Houston Grand Opera); *Rape of Lucretia* (Sydney Chamber Opera/Victorian Opera); *A Midsummer Night's Dream* (Chicago Lyric Opera/Houston Grand Opera/Canadian Opera Company); *The Magic Flute* (Lyric Opera Chicago); and *Chorus!* (Houston Grand Opera). His designs for dance include *The Narrative of Nothing*, *Firebird*, *Swan Lake* (Australian Ballet); *Am I* (Shaun Parker & Company); *Affinity* (Tasdance); *Mortal Engine* (Chunky Move); *Of Earth and Sky* (Bangarra Dance Theatre); and *Orb* (Sydney Dance Company). For lighting design, Damien has won three Sydney Theatre Awards, three Green Room Awards, and two Australian Production Design Guild Awards.

HARRY COVILL Composer & Sound Designer

Harry creates eclectic music and sound design for screen and live performance. In 2017, he graduated from VCA majoring in Interactive Composition. His recent work includes composing, recording and mixing the original score for the feature film *Girl Asleep* directed by Rosemary Myers (nominated for seven AACTA Awards) and short film *A Field Guide to Being a 12-Year-Old Girl* directed by Tilda Cobham-Hervey for ABC TV. In January, he created the sound design for *Last Active*, a multiscreen exhibition held at the ACMI. He has also recently collaborated with director Bruce Gladwin at Back to Back Theatre, writing original scores for the internationally acclaimed art project *Democratic Set*. In late 2016 Harry devised, recorded and composed the score for Theatre of Speed's music video *Radial*. Prior to this he created the score and sound design for Windmill Theatre Company's production *Big Bad Wolf*, which undertook a 16-city tour of North America and has also enjoyed seasons at Melbourne Theatre Company, Queensland Performing Arts Centre, and the Perth Awesome Festival.

Matthew Whittet & Lucia Mastrantone

GEORGIANE DEAL Assistant Stage Manager

Georgiane completed a Bachelor of Dramatic Art (Production) at Excelsia College (2014). She has worked in stage management for various theatre and live events, most recently *The Secret River* (Sydney Theatre Company); *The Rape of Lucretia, Biographica* (Sydney Chamber Opera); *The Caucasian Chalk* Circle (NIDA); *Neighbourhood Watch, Life Without Me* (Illuminate Educate); *The Screwtape Letters* (Clock & Spiel); *Journey's End* and *The Block Universe* (Cross Pollinate). Georgiane is thrilled to work on her first Belvoir show with *Atlantis*.

LUCIA MASTRANTONE Bella, New York Taxi Driver, Dossie & Others

Lucia has a successful career in theatre, physical theatre, film, television and as a voice artist. She has worked for many major theatre companies including Belvoir where her credits include *Twelfth Night or What You Will*, *The Book of Everything*, *Scorched*, *Macbeth*, *My Vicious Angel*, *The Popular Mechanicals 1 & 2* and *Love and Magic in Mama's Kitchen*. Lucia was Associate Director for Belvoir's acclaimed *Baulkham Hills African Ladies Troupe*. Other theatre credits include *Talk, Marriage Blanc, Romeo and Juliet* (Sydney Theatre Company); *The Duchess of Malfi* (Bell Shakespeare); *Ladies Day* (Griffin); *The Merchant of Venice, Six Characters In Search Of An Author, A Little Like Drowning, The Rover* (State Theatre Company South Australia); and *Venetian Twins* (Melbourne Theatre Company). Lucia's physical theatre credits include *Under the Influence* (Legs on the Wall, European, Edinburgh tour and Belvoir season); *Verona, Little Miss Hood* (Magpie Theatre/Melbourne Theatre Company); *Blue Love* (Shaun Parker Company, Australian and German tour); *The Longest Night* (Urban Theatre Projects commissioned by Peter Sellers, Adelaide Festival); *Running Show* (NYID, European tour); and *Ricordi* (Doppio Teatro, UK Tour). Her vocal work has involved several plays and book readings for ABC Radio National, the children's movie *Napoleon*, and she is currently a co-star in Working Dog's hit TV animation series *Pacific Heat*. Lucia's screen credits include the television series *Tangle, Rake* and *Home and Away*, and the AFI Award-winning films *Look Both Ways* and *Bad Boy Bubby*.

AMBER McMAHON Lally Katz

Amber graduated from Flinders University Drama Centre in 2002 and has since worked across the country and abroad with a host of leading companies. For Belvoir, Amber has appeared in *Girl Asleep* (Windmill Theatre Company); *Twelfth Night or What You Will*, *Angels in America Parts One* and *Two* and *The Power of Yes*. Amber's other recent theatre credits include *Picnic at Hanging Rock* (Malthouse Theatre/Edinburgh Tour); *The Popular Mechanicals* (State Theatre Company South Australia/Sydney Theatre Company); *Tribes* (Ensemble); *North by Northwest* (Melbourne Theatre Company); *Optimism* (Malthouse Theatre); and *School Dance* (Windmill Theatre Company). She was also a founding member of STC's Actors Ensemble, appearing in several productions including *The War of the Roses*, *Gallipoli*, *The Lost Echo* and *The Season at Sarsaparilla*. Amber has twice won the Helpmann Award for Best Female Actor in a Supporting Role, for her performance in *Girl Asleep* and *School Dance*. She appeared in Windmill's film adaptation of *Girl Asleep*, directed by Rosemary Myers. Amber has also written stand-up for corporate, political and creative events as her character Audrey.

JONATHON OXLADE Set & Costume Designer

Jonathon studied Illustration and Sculpture at the Queensland College of Art. He has designed set and costumes for Belvoir, State Theatre Company South Australia, Windmill Theatre Company, Queensland Theatre Company, Dead Puppet Society, Is This Yours?, Aphids, Circa, Arena Theatre Company, Polyglot, Bell Shakespeare, Polytoxic, Men of Steel, The Real TV Project, Lemony S Puppet Theatre, Terrapin Puppet Theatre, Vitalstatistix, Barking Gecko, The Border Project, Sydney Theatre Company, LaBoite Theatre and The Escapists. Jonathon has illustrated the picture book *The Empty City* for Hachette Livre/Lothian and the *Edie Amelia* series by Sophie Lee, was festival designer for the Out of the Box Festival in 2010 and Brisbane Festival's ARCADIA in 2015, and is currently the Resident Designer at Windmill. Jonathon has received Matilda Awards for Best Designer for *A Christmas Carol* and Contribution to Queensland Theatre in 2005, and Best Designer for *Attack of the Attacking Attackers* in 2009. He was nominated for a Green Room Award in 2010 for *Goodbye Vaudeville Charlie Mudd*, and won a Ruby Award in 2011 for *School Dance*. Jonathon was also nominated for Helpmann Awards in 2013 and 2014 for *School Dance* and *Pinocchio*, along with Green Room nominations in 2014 and 2015 for *Skeleton* and *I Heart John McEnroe*. Jonathon worked as production and costume designer on *Girl Asleep*, Windmill's premiere feature film, for which he won an AACTA Award for Best Costume Design. Jonathon was awarded the Lord Mayors Fellowship Grant to attend the Prague Quadrennial of Scenography and Theatre Architecture, and is a 2017 Sidney Myer Creative Fellow.

HAZEM SHAMMAS Diego, Panther & Others

Since graduating from WAAPA, **Hazem** has worked on many productions with major theatre companies in Australia. His theatre credits include *Mother Courage and Her Children*, *Scorched*, *Antigone*, *Paul*, *Gates of Egypt*, *Peribanez*, *Stuff Happens* (Belvoir); *Disgraced* (Melbourne Theatre Company); *Othello* (State Theatre Company South Australia); *The Tempest*, *A Comedy of Errors*, *Macbeth* (Bell Shakespeare); *The Call* (Griffin); *Criminology* (Malthouse Theatre); *A Midsummer Night's Dream* (Arts Radar); *The Tribe* and *Buried City* (UTP/Belvoir/Sydney Festival). Hazem's screen credits include *Underbelly*, *East West 101*, *At Home With Julia*, *All Saints*, the upcoming mini-series *Safe Harbour*, and the feature films *X*, *The Tumbler* and *Alex and Eve*. Hazem is also a founder and director of Poetry in Action, a national touring theatre-in-education company that teaches poetry, literacy and the arts to high school students across the country.

KEIREN SMITH Stage Manager

For Belvoir, **Keiren** has been stage manager on *La Traviata* and assistant stage manager on *Hir*, *Mark Colvin's Kidney*, *The Drover's Wife*, *Back at the Dojo*, *Mother Courage and Her Children*, *Radiance*, *Nora*, *Brothers Wreck* and *Once in Royal David's City*. She has an Advanced Diploma in Stage Management from WAAPA and a Bachelor of Arts in Communication and Cultural Studies from Curtin University. Keiren was assistant stage manager with The Australian Ballet for three years, touring domestically and internationally including to Japan and New York, working on many repertoire and new ballets such as *Don Quixote*, *Onegin*, *The Merry Widow*, *Madame Butterfly*, *Coppelia*, *The Nutcracker*, *The Silver Rose*, Alexei Ratmansky's *Cinderella*, Stephen Bayne's *Swan Lake* and Graeme Murphy's *Romeo and Juliet*. She has stage managed *I Love You Now* (Darlinghurst Theatre Co) and was assistant stage manager on *Theodora* (Pinchgut Opera); *Hay Fever* (Sydney Theatre Company); *Solomon and Marion* (Melbourne Theatre Company); *The Web*, *Much Ado About Nothing* (Black Swan); and Sydney New Year's Eve – Lord Mayor's Party (City of Sydney).

PAIGE WALKER Dialect Coach

Paige has 27 years' experience in the industry, ranging from theatre and dance to voiceovers and aerial work, but her work as a dialect coach has been some of her most fulfilling. For Belvoir, she has been dialect coach on *Hir*, *Mr Burns*, and the Helpmann Award-winning *The Glass Menagerie* and *Angels in America Parts One* and *Two*. Other recent credits include *Disgraced* and *Testament of Mary* (Sydney Theatre Company), and *Beautiful: The Carole King Musical*. Paige is a US native and began her life in the arts at one of the country's leading performing arts schools. Following on from there she received her Bachelor of Fine Arts in Theatre before heading off to tread the boards in New York. In 2000, Paige made the journey to Australia and began teaching American dialect full time. Her coaching has seen her work with artists including Stef Dawson, Dan Mor, Hugh Sheridan, Jodi Gordon, Andy Whitfield, Delta Goodrem and Jessica Mauboy.

MATTHEW WHITTET Dave, Pop-Op, Bella's Daughter & Others

Matthew is an actor and writer who has worked extensively in theatre, film and television for the past 19 years. Matt has performed extensively across Australia for companies including Belvoir, Windmill Theatre Company, Sydney Theatre Company, Malthouse Theatre, Bell Shakespeare and State Theatre Company South Australia, with directors such as Rosemary Myers, Neil Armfield, Barrie Kosky, Benedict Andrews and Michael Kantor. As an actor, Matt has performed for Belvoir many times, most recently in *Girl Asleep*, *Cinderella*, *The Book Of Everything* and *Conversation Piece*. His film credits include *Girl Asleep*, *The Great Gatsby*, *Australia*, *You Can't Stop The Murders* and *Moulin Rouge!*. As a writer, Matt's plays for Belvoir include *Seventeen* (which recently played at the Lyric Theatre in London), *Cinderella*, *Old Man* and *Silver*. Matt's collaboration with Windmill Theatre Co has resulted in four plays: *Girl Asleep, School Dance, Big Bad Wolf* and *Fugitive*. Matt's award-winning feature film adaptation of his play *Girl Asleep* (supported by the Hive Production Fund) debuted at the Adelaide Film Festival and went on to open the 2016 Generation 14 Plus Program at the Berlin International Film Festival. Matt was among the seven Sidney Myer Creative Fellows chosen in 2012.

Paula Arundell

Amber McMahon

Hazem Shammas

Matthew Whittet &
Amber McMahon

BELVOIR STAFF

18 Belvoir Street, Surry Hills NSW 2010
Email mail@belvoir.com.au Web belvoir.com.au
Administration (02) 9698 3344 Facsimile (02) 9319 3165 Box Office (02) 9699 3444

Artistic Director
Eamon Flack
Executive Director
Sue Donnelly
Deputy Executive Director & Head of Development
Aaron Beach

BELVOIR BOARD
Patricia Akopiantz
Mitchell Butel
Luke Carroll
Sue Donnelly
Tracey Driver
Eamon Flack
Ian Learmonth
Michael Lynch
Sam Meers (Chair)
Peter Wilson

BELVOIR ST THEATRE BOARD
Stuart McCreery
Angela Pearman (Chair)
Sue Rosen
Nick Schlieper
Mark Seymour
Kingsley Slipper
Susan Teasey

ARTISTIC & PROGRAMMING
Associate Director – New Work
Anthea Williams
Artistic Associate
Tom Wright
Associate Artist
Tessa Leong
Associate Producer
Dom Mercer

EDUCATION
Education Manager
Jane May
Education Coordinator
Sharon Zeeman

ADMINISTRATION
Company Manager
Matthew Rossi
Office Manager
Jessica Vincent

FINANCE & OPERATIONS
Company Accountant
Barbara Lewis
Accounts Administrator
Susan Jack
Venue Hire Manager
Caitlin Porter

MARKETING
Head of Marketing & Customer Service
Amy Goodhew
Marketing Coordinator
Georgia Goode
Communications Coordinator
Cara Nash

BOX OFFICE & CUSTOMER SERVICES
Customer Experience & Ticketing Manager
Andrew Dillon
Ticketing Systems Administrator
Tanya Ginori-Cairns
CRM Manager
Charlotte Bradley
Customer Service Coordinator
Anna Booty
Guest Operations Coordinator
Keila Terencio

FRONT OF HOUSE
Front of House Manager
Scott Pirlo
Assistant Front of House Manager
Luke Martin

DEVELOPMENT
Philanthropy Managers
Joanna Maunder & Liz Tomkinson
Development Coordinator
Kseniia Grishilova

PRODUCTION
Head of Production
Sally Withnell
Technical Manager
Aiden Brennan
Deputy Production Manager
Roxzan Bowes
Senior Technician
Raine Paul
Resident Stage Manager
Luke McGettigan
Staging & Construction Manager
Penny Angrick
Staging & Construction Assistant
Brydie Ryan
Costume Coordinator
Judy Tanner
Commercial Construction Managers
Simon Boyd & Brett Wilbe

BELVOIR 2018

MY NAME IS JIMI
5 – 21 JANUARY

SINGLE ASIAN FEMALE
16 FEBRUARY – 25 MARCH

SAMI IN PARADISE
1 – 29 APRIL

THE SUGAR HOUSE
5 MAY – 8 JUNE

BLISS
9 JUNE – 15 JULY

A TASTE OF HONEY
21 JULY – 19 AUGUST

CALAMITY JANE
23 AUGUST – 30 SEPTEMBER

AN ENEMY OF THE PEOPLE
7 OCTOBER – 4 NOVEMBER

THE DANCE OF DEATH
10 NOVEMBER – 23 DECEMBER

MY URRWAI
18 JANUARY – 4 FEBRUARY

MOTHER
24 JANUARY – 11 FEBRUARY

BELVOIR HA HA
1 – 4 FEBRUARY

RANDOM
18 OCTOBER – 11 NOVEMBER

SUBSCRIBE NOW
BELVOIR.COM.AU

BELVOIR

THEATRICALITY.
VARIETY OF LIFE.
FAITH IN HUMANITY.

Belvoir is a theatre company on a side street in Surry Hills, Sydney. We share our street with a park and a public housing estate, and our theatre is in an old industrial building. It has been, at various times, a garage, a sauce factory, and the Nimrod Theatre. When the theatre was threatened with redevelopment in 1984, more than 600 people formed a syndicate to buy the building and save the theatre. Thirty years later, Belvoir St Theatre continues to be home to one of Australia's most celebrated theatre companies.

In its early years Belvoir was run cooperatively. It later rose to international prominence under first and longest-serving Artistic Director Neil Armfield and continued to be both wildly successful and controversial under Ralph Myers. Belvoir is a traditional home for the great old crafts of acting and story in Australian theatre. It is a platform for voices that won't otherwise be heard. And it is a gathering of outspoken ideals. In short: theatricality, variety of life, and faith in humanity.

At Belvoir we gather the best theatre artists we can find, emerging and established, to realise an annual season of works – new Australian plays, Indigenous works, re-imagined classics and new international writing. Audiences remember many landmark productions including *The Drover's Wife*, *Angels in America*, *Brothers Wreck*, *The Glass Menagerie*, *Neighbourhood Watch*, *The Wild Duck*, *Medea*, *The Diary of a Madman*, *Death of a Salesman*, *The Blind Giant is Dancing*, *Hamlet*, *Cloudstreet*, *Aliwa*, *The Book of Everything*, *Keating!*, *The Exile Trilogy*, *Exit the King*, *The Sapphires*, *The Rover*, *Faith Healer* and many more.

Today, under Artistic Director Eamon Flack and Executive Director Sue Donnelly, Belvoir tours nationally and internationally, and continues to create its own brand of rough magic for new generations of audiences.

Belvoir receives government support for its activities from the federal government through the Major Performing Arts Panel of the Australia Council and the state government through Arts NSW. We also welcome and warmly appreciate all philanthropic support.

belvoir.com.au

BELVOIR DONORS

We give our heartfelt thanks to all our donors for their loyal and generous support.

CREATIVE DEVELOPMENT FUND

$10,000+
Stephen Allen
Andrew Cameron AM & Cathy Cameron**
Helen Lynch AM & Helen Bauer**
Frank Macindoe*
Sherry-Hogan Foundation*
Kim Williams AM & Catherine Dovey

$5,000 – $9,999
Anonymous (1)
Jill & Richard Berry
Anne Britton**
Hartley Cook*
Louise Herron AM & Clark Butler**
Peter & Rosemary Ingle*
Don & Leslie Parsonage
Dan & Jackie Phillips
Doc Ross Family Foundation
Victoria Taylor**
Shemara Wikramanayake & Ed Gilmartin

$2,000 – $4,999
Neil Armfield AO**
Justin Butterworth
John Cary
Janet & Trefor Clayton*
Michael Coleman*
Victoria Holthouse*

$500 – $1,999
Robert Crossman
Richard Evans
Ross McLean & Fiona Beith*
Louise & Michael Nettleton
Angela Pearman
Steve & Belinda Rankine
Richard, Heather & Rachel Rasker
Sally & Jonathan Rourke
Mark Warburton
Penny Ward

CO-CONSPIRATORS

$10,000+
Gail Hambly**
Anita Jacoby*
Sam Meers
David Pumphrey
Mark Warburton
Peter Wilson & James Emmett
Cathy Yuncken

B KEEPERS

$5,000+
Robert & Libby Albert**
Ellen Borda*
Constructability Recruitment
Marion Heathcote & Brian Burfitt**
Bruce Meagher & Greg Waters
Don & Leslie Parsonage*
Jann Skinner

$3,000 – $4,999
Anonymous (1)
Anne Britton**
Louise Christie**
Tom Dent
Suzanne & Michael Daniel**
Bob & Chris Ernst**
David & Kathryn Groves*
Judge Joe Harman
Marion Heathcote & Brian Burfitt**
Michael Hobbs**
Colleen Kane**
Tony Maxwell & Robyn Godlee
Chantal & Greg Roger**
Michael Rose
Lesley & Andrew Rosenberg*
Peter & Jan Shuttleworth*
Merilyn Sleigh & Raoul de Ferranti
Patricia Wong

$2,000 – $2,999
Antoinette Albert**
Claire Armstrong & John Sharpe**
Charlene & Graham Bradley AM
Jillian Broadbent AO**
Chris Brown
Jan Burnswoods*
Dr. Kimberly Cartwright & Mr. Charles Littrell
Jan Chapman AO & Stephen O'Rourke
Wesley Enoch
Danny & Kathleen Gilbert**
Cary & Rob Gillespie
Sophie Guest
Peter Graves**
David Haertsch**
John Head**
Libby Higgin*
Jennifer Ledgar & Bob Lim*
Louise Mitchell & Peter Pether
Professor Elizabeth More AM**
Dr David Nguyen**
Timothy & Eva Pascoe**

David & Emma Scambler
Ann Sherry AO*
Judy Thomson*
Lynne Watkins & Nicholas Harding*

$1,000 – $1,999
Anonymous (2)
Berg Family Foundation**
Allen & Julie Blewitt
Jake Blundell
Max Bonnell**
Dr Catherine Brown-Watt PSM
Mary Jo & Lloyd Capps**
Jane Christensen*
Annabel Crabb & Jeremy Storer
Jeanne Eve**
Lisa Hamilton & Rob White
Wendy & Andrew Hamlin**
Susan Ingram
Avril Jeans**
Kevin & Rosemarie Jeffers-Palmer ***
Corinne & Rob Johnston*
Margaret Johnston
A. le Marchant*
Stephanie Lee*
Atul Lele*
Hilary Linstead**
Louise McBride
Ross McLean & Fiona Beith*
Cajetan Mula (Honorary Member)
K Nomchong SC
Anthony Nugent
Jacqueline & Michael Palmer
Dr Natalie Pelham*
Greeba Pritchard*
David & Jill Pumphrey
Richard, Heather & Rachel Rasker*
Alex Oonagh Redmond**
Richmond Sisters
Colleen Roche
David Round
Andrew & Louise Sharpe*
Jennifer Smith
Chris & Bea Sochan*
Camilla & Andrew Strang
Sue Thomson*
Alese Watson
Paul & Jennifer Winch

THE HIVE

$2,500
Elizabeth Allen & David Langley
Anthony & Elly Baxter
Aaron Beach & Deborah Brown

Nathan & Yael Bennett
Justin Butterworth
Dan & Emma Chesterman
Este Darin-Cooper & Chris Burgess
Joanna Davidson & Julian Leeser
Tracey Driver
Piers Grove
Ruth Higgins & Tamson Pietsch
David Rayment & Mary Nguyen
Hannah Roache & Luke Turner
Andrew & Louise Sharpe*
Chris Smith
The Sky Foundation
Peter Wilson & James Emmett

HONEY Bs
$1,000+
Margaret Butler
Marla Heller
Tristan Landers
Louise McCoach
Olivia Pascoe
Janet Pennington
Sylvia Preda
Janna Robertson
Arlene Tansey
Lauren Thompson
Cathy Yuncken

EDUCATION DONORS
$10,000+
Doc Ross Family Foundation
Susie & Nick Kelly
Ian Learmonth & Julia Pincus

$5,000 - $9,999
Margaret Butler
Kimberly & Angus Holden
Veronica & Matthew Latham
Rob Thomas

$2,000 – $4,999
Anonymous (3)
Andrew Cameron AM & Cathy Cameron**
Estate of the late Angelo Comino
John B Fairfax AO & Libby Fairfax
Ari Droga
Julie Hannaford*
Judge Joe Harman
Bill Hawker
David Jonas & Desmon Du Plessis

$500 – $1,999
Anonymous (4)
32 Edward St
Len & Nita Armfield
AB*
Arrow Commodities

Ian Barnett*
Jessica Block
Sue Capon
Michael & Colleen Chesterman*
Erin Devery
Denise & Robert Dunn
Susan Gabriel
Geoffrey & Patricia Gemmell*
Peter Gray
Dorothy Hoddinott AO**
Sue Hyde*
Peter & Rosemary Ingle*
Catherine Jones
Ruth Layton
Annabelle Mahar
Christopher Matthies
Mary Miltenyi
Patricia Novikoff
Nicole Philps
Plaza Films
Polese Family
Richard, Heather & Rachel Rasker
Angela Raymond
Geoffrey Rush AC
Julianne Schultz
Peter & Janet Shuttleworth*
Chris & Bea Sochan*
Dr Titia Sprague
Cheri Stevenson
Kerry Stubbs
Daniela Torsh

GENERAL DONORS
$10,000+
Anonymous (1)
Andrew Cameron AM & Cathy Cameron**
Dr Kimberly Cartwright & Mr Charles Littrell
Ross Littlewood & Alexandra Curtin*

$2,000 – $4,999
Anonymous (2)
Samantha Acret
Brenna Hobson
Raymond McDonald
Ralph Myers
Timothy & Eva Pascoe
Lynne Watkins & Nicolas Harding*

$500 – $1,999
Anonymous (9)
Annette Adair
Victor Baskir
Baiba Berzins*
Christine Bishop
Mr Dennis Bluth & Dr Diana Marks
Keith Bradley AM
Ian Breden & Josephine Key*
Anne Britton**

Robert Burns
Colleen & Michael Chesterman
Tim & Bryony Cox*
Jane Diamond*
Camilla Done
Jane Mary Eagger
Anton Enus
Gillian Fenton
Sandra Ferman
Tim Gerrard
Verity Goitein
Peter Gray & Helen Thwaites
Priscilla Guest*
Dr Cheryl Hanbury
Grania Hickley
Ruth Higgins & Tamson Pietsch
Dorothy Hoddinott AO**
Clyth Hoult
Robert Kidd
Cheryl L
Connie Liu
Lisa Manchur
Julianne Maxwell
E.J.R McDonald
Irene Miller*
Peter Mitchell
Patricia Novikoff*
Judy & Geoff Patterson*
Christina Pender
Susan Pugh
Kim Rosser
Leigh Sanderson
Elfriede Sangkuhl
Dr Agnes Sinclair
Eileen Slarke & Family**
Andrea Socratous
Paul Stein
Leslie Stern
Yael Stone
Axel & Diane Tennie
Mike Thompson
Tom Tilley
Helen Trinca
Suzanne & Ross Tzannes AM*
Jane Uebergang
Louise & Steve Verrier
Chris Vik & Chelsea Albert
Sarah Walters*
Louisa Ward & Tim Coen
Elizabeth Webby AM
Dr Rosemary White
Brian & Trish Wright
Carolyn Wright

* 5+ years of giving
** 10+ years of giving
*** 15+ years of giving
List correct at time of printing.

Belvoir is very grateful to accept donations of all sizes. Donations over $2 are tax deductible. If you would like to make a donation or would like further information about any of our donor programs please call our Development Team on 02 9698 3344 or email development@belvoir.com.au

BELVOIR DONORS *Continued*

SPECIAL THANKS

We would like to acknowledge Cajetan Mula, Len Armfield and Geoffrey Scharer. They will always be remembered for their generosity to Belvoir.

We also thank our Life Members, who have made outstanding contributions to Belvoir over more than thirty years. They have changed the course of the company and are now ingrained in its fabric: Neil Armfield AO, Neil Balnaves AO, Andrew Cameron AM, David Gonski AC, Rachel Healy, Louise Herron AM, Sue Hill, Geoffrey Rush AC, Orli Wargon OAM and Chris Westwood.

These people and foundations supported the redevelopment of Belvoir St Theatre and purchase of our warehouse.

Andrew & Cathy Cameron
(refurbishment of theatre & warehouse)

Russell Crowe
(Downstairs theatre &
purchase of warehouse)

The Gonski Foundation
& Nelson Meers Foundation
(Gonski Meers Foyer)

Andrew & Wendy Hamlin
(Brenna's office)

Hal Herron
(The Hal Bar)

Geoffrey Rush
(redevelopment of theatre)

Fred Street AM
(Upstairs dressing room)

THE TRUTH WILL COME TO LIGHT
New Australian Drama
Sunshine
Complete Season Now Streaming
Starring Anthony LaPaglia
SBS ON DEMAND

CLUB DENDY

LOVE MOVIES? COME AND JOIN OUR CLUB TO ACCESS THESE AMAZING BENEFITS AND MORE!

 Discounted movie tickets for you and a guest all year round!

 Access to exclusive screenings and preview events

 10% off the Candy Bar *excluding alcohol

 Exclusive offers and weekly upates

 See four movies, get the fifth free!

 Our partners will treat you too

Visit www.dendy.com.au/club-dendy for more info.

DENDY CINEMAS

PROUDLY SUPPORTING BELVOIR*

*EP

EP is the leading TV, Media & Entertainment Recuitment and Executive Search Firm
Fox Studios Australia | epaustralia.com.au | 02 9383 4520

HANDPICKED WINES

SYDNEY URBAN CELLAR DOOR
Your Destination for Australian Wine Education & Experiences

50 KENSINGTON STREET, CHIPPENDALE 2008 | www.handpickedwines.com.au | @handpickedwines

VINI

PROUD SUPPORTER OF BELVOIR

ITALIAN FOOD & WINE
3/118 DEVONSHIRE ST (ON HOLT)
SURRY HILLS 9698 5131
Now open Monday nights!

Mon 5:30pm - late
Tues to Thurs 6pm - late
Fri noon - late
Sat 5:30pm - late
WWW.VINI.COM.AU

Ticket holders receive complimentary crostini of the day.

BELVOIR SUPPORTERS

Our patrons, supporters and friends are right there behind us, backing Belvoir in bringing to life the great old theatrical crafts of acting and storytelling. Thank you.

Learn more about supporting Belvoir at belvoir.com.au/support-belvoir

KEY SUPPORTER

Indigenous theatre at Belvoir supported by The Balnaves Foundation

TRUSTS & FOUNDATIONS

Andrew Cameron Family Foundation
Coca-Cola Foundation
Gandevia Foundation
The Greatorex Foundation
Macquarie Group Foundation
Nelson Meers Foundation
Teen Spirit Charitable Foundation
Thyne Reid Foundation
Walking up The Hill Foundation

BELVOIR PARTNERS

GOVERNMENT PARTNERS

YOUTH & EDUCATION PARTNER

MAJOR PARTNERS

ASSOCIATE PARTNERS

SUPPORTING PARTNER

MEDIA PARTNERS

PRODUCTION PARTNER

IT PARTNER

EVENT PARTNERS

For more information on partnership opportunities please contact our Development team on 02 9698 3344 or email development@belvoir.com.au

Correct at time of printing.

www.ingramcontent.com/pod-product-compliance
Lightning Source LLC
Chambersburg PA
CBHW050017090426
42734CB00021B/3299